Searching for Serenity

in My Crazy Life

ELLY STEVENS

Searching for Serenity in My Crazy Life, the real-life stories of a baby boomer from the city of Rochester, New York, from 1948 to 2018.

Dedicated to my

beautiful granddaughter

Amanda D. Stevens

Introduction

WE WERE UNIQUE. I was born Eloise Mae Fedyk, the middle child in a family of 5 children, in April 1948, and grew up on an inner-city street, Baumann Street, which had a "steep" hill (steep to us kids), a rare occurrence in Rochester, NY. It was great for riding sleds down the hill, or riding car bumpers up the hill (I didn't do that, of course). In the olden days, the middle daughter would have the prestigious job of walking the family cow up Baumann Hill to the pasture. I never saw any cows on our street in my day, but I did hear roosters crowing at the break of dawn on summer mornings. I think they lived on Dayton Street.

WE WERE RICH. Or, at least I thought we were. Dad (James Fedyk) worked at Kodak and made lenses for secret government missions and later NASA, and every Friday at noon Mom (Helen) would drive to the Hawkeye Plant to pick up his paycheck. After I rolled down the hill on someone's property several times, because I could, not because I asked permission, Dad would come to the car and hand over a large check to my mom and sometimes he'd bring out a candy bar for me from his vending machine. And every Friday night, we'd have a haddock fish fry from Charlie's corner bar on Avenue D or Otto's Tavern on Remington Street. That was living it up, yes sirree, Bob!

WE WERE CULTURED. Our house was centered in four ethnic neighborhoods.

- On the southwest side (Joseph Avenue) was the Jewish community with their bakeries (esp. Bodner's), fishmongers, Blank's butcher shop, Bless' drug store, Buster Brown shoe store, Lotz hardware, and a temple.

- On the northwest side (again, Joseph Avenue) was the German community, with their sausage shops and delis, the former Scheutzen Park, and, of course, their bars (e.g., Otto's Tavern). I went to a German school and church, Our Lady of Perpetual Help (OLPH), although I never heard any German there. It was the parish of my Polish grandparents, Lawrence and Mary (Kujawa) Littlebetter who lived nearby on VanStallen Street.

- On the southeast side was the Polish community (Hudson Avenue) with their bakery (Wojtczak's), sausage shops, ice cream parlor (Andy's Candies), and numerous bars. They also had the best library in the city, the Pulaski Library. We were mostly Polish, but did not attend the Polish parish, St. Stanislaus.

- And lastly, on the northeast side was the Ukrainian community (also Hudson Avenue) with Habza's sausage shop and Wandkte's bar and restaurant. (People ate a lot of sausage and drank a lot of beer back then.) Our dentist, Dr. Kindrat, also had his practice there. Hung in his waiting room were pictures of several bearded Russians, which scared all the little kids. My father was officially part of the Eastern Rite Ukrainian church, St. Josaphat's, but we attended Mom's parish because of her devotion to it and that's where she went to grammar school.

Dad often took us around "his" city to show us places and things of the soon-to-be past, like Front Street, where drunks slept in doorways and the buildings were practically falling into the Genesee River. He also took us to the art and the science museums to expose us to culture, refinement (haha), and history.

WE WERE TALENTED. Dad was a good artist and taught us how to draw in "point perspective." My older sister Marcia was a natural artist, as well, and a soprano, pianist, and avid reader. Mom was good with words, and could time herself on the most difficult crossword. She was an avid reader, too, and was very interested in Extra Sensory Perception. (She saw the ghost of her grandmother, immediately after her death, coming down the stairs.) My older brother James (Jimmy) died at age 10, but I know he was smart and loved TV cowboys and his extensive train setup in the basement. I wrote stories and plays, even at the age of 6 or 7, and shared Mom's love of words and ESP. I also took piano lessons, but that was short-lived when Sister Carlotta smacked my knuckles with a pointer. My younger brother Michael (we called him Mickey) and my younger sister Patricia (Patty) arrived 10 and 11 years later after me, respectively, with their own talents. Mickey acted and sang in several Gilbert & Sullivan plays, and Patty took dance lessons, enjoyed art, studied ESP, and collected rocks. (Nothing as exciting as finding a geode!)

WE WERE FUN. Dad was the first one in the neighborhood to own a TV set. I never remember life without one. Dad was also proud of his Webcor Hi-Fi. Blasting his Hi-Fi. He had to have the very latest "stereo sampler," like the one with Bob & Ray, a comedy act. Everyone on the street knew when he was home from work. And we always had a summer vacation, whether at Honeoye Lake, the 1,000 Islands, Beaver Lake in Canada, Niagara Falls, "The Millionaire's Club" in Clayton, New York, and memorable trips to Albany, Cooperstown, and Howe Caverns. Family and friends would polka in our tiny kitchen (hoopa, shoopa!), and we would celebrate anniversaries, First Communions, graduations, etc., with an outdoor party. Of course, the children went off and played while the adults partied with lots of beer and sausage and listened to Dad's stereo blasting.

WE WERE WILD AND FREE. No one kept tabs on us kids. If I decided to walk to my cousin Bonnie's house in Irondequoit by the beach, I just went. (Then I'd call my mom and ask if I could stay overnight.) If we wanted to see a movie, we took a bus downtown to the RKO Palace or we'd walk to the Sun Theater on Joseph Avenue and stay all afternoon. If I wanted to have lunch at my grandma's, I would stop there during my lunch break. (We had to walk home for lunch every day during grammar school.) If my friends wanted to walk to Seneca Park to catch tadpoles, I'd just go with them. If we wanted an apple off a stranger's tree, we'd just take one. We were encouraged to go to the library, which we did every Saturday, to bring home an armload of books. Our only rule was: when it was dark and the street lights came on, we were supposed to be home.

Now that you know a little bit about my background, I hope you will enjoy my true stories, happy and sad, silly and shocking. It's just who I am.

Elly

Life on Baumann Street

Rochester, NY

1948-1968

.

Early Memories and Mom's Family

I REALLY DO REMEMBER being in my crib. It was pushed against an inner wall in my sister Marcia's bedroom, next to the heating vent. The vent was also connected to the bathroom, which was not pleasant after the adults had beer and sausage.

My hair was mousy brown with some red and gold highlights and I had brown eyes. Mom used to sing, *"Beautiful, beautiful brown eyes. I'll never love blue eyes again,"* to lull me to sleep. But all the brown seemed to make me invisible when I wanted lots of attention.

Dad named me Eloise, after his dentist's sister. He liked the name, which means "Famous in battle." Very *apropos.* I was an awful kid. (Actually, we all were wild and unruly.) My family called me "Ella" or "Ella Bella Marie" or "Eloweezer is a geezer." I hated my name.

Mom was a gentle soul, a hard-working housewife, very religious, and very careful with money down to the penny, but she always financially supported our church, school, and missions around the world where people were starving. I clung to Mom like glue whenever we went anywhere. She wished I didn't hang on the arm that picked up her beer glass, though.

Mom with Marcia, Jimmy and Me

Dad had a strong personality. He'd say to my Uncle John, "You and I are perfect, but sometimes I wonder about you." It was always his way or no way. Sometimes he'd joke; but sometimes he'd be dead serious. It was often hard to tell the difference, and many times I read him wrong and ended up being sent to my room or worse, got the "belt."

Mom was a Democrat but Dad was a Republican. They never saw eye to eye. Mom usually kept her beliefs to herself unless something happened that truly upset her, and then there were tears shed. Dad had no empathy. After all, he was "perfect."

My greatest fear as a baby and toddler was being left alone or abandoned. I don't know why. If Mom wanted to go downtown on the bus and I found out about it, holy hell would break loose. I'd cry and scratch and kick and bite. Not a good way to convince someone to take me along. Once, she left me with Grandma Littlebetter and, I hate to admit it, I was like a wild cat. Poor, gentle Grandma. She would just say in Polish, *"o jejku kochany!"* ("Oh, my goodness!"). Another time, Mom had a shopping day planned, so she came to my crib and promised to buy me my very own pillow (bribery!). I never had a pillow before, so I decided to play nice and get the pillow, which I did. I was very proud of my "big-girl" possession.

As I grew older, I didn't change much. I was a "brat," or as Marcia called me, "a snot." We had to share a double bed, which had a chenille bedspread, but sometimes we'd fight over the covers and Marcia would have bloody scratches from my fingernails and toenails.

When Marcia started taking piano lessons, she brought home her new practice book and I promptly scribbled crayon all over it. The next day, Sister Carlotta asked her why she scribbled on her new book. She said, "The baby did it." Yup, it was a masterpiece.

I also got into Mom's purse one day, during one of her social functions in the backyard. Her bright red lipstick nicely decorated everything in her purse, including all the family photos in her wallet. They are still red today.

Marcia was eight years older than I, loved fashion, singing, piano, art, reading books, and swimming. So talented! She also had JEWELRY and perfume. I loved looking at all the sparkly items in her jewelry box and trying them on when she wasn't home. She had the most fashionable clothes for the 1950s! A few things ended up in my closet. I got some of her hand-me down clothing, and she got some hand-me-downs from Aunt Joanne, so nothing went to the "ragman" until it was truly rags.

Since I am a "baby boomer," we were inundated with World War II shows on TV, like *Victory at Sea*. Marcia invented a playtime activity called "Escape from Hamburg" in which we were imprisoned in cages and fed rotten bananas. Then we "escaped" by jumping from twin bed to twin bed upstairs, or couch to chair downstairs. Because I was little, I told Mom we were playing "Steak from Hamburg." She couldn't figure out what I was talking about! Marcia just laughed.

Another favorite playtime for me was playing "birds" and "horses" with my best friend, Judy Gekoski, who lived across the street, mainly because she loved them so much. As birds, we flew around the yard looking for worms and feeding our young. As horses, we galloped in the yard with our hands behind us, neighing and whinnying, eating hay, and pretending people were riding us and getting thrown off. Such fun. Dad watched us from the kitchen window, laughing and calling us "nuts."

When I went to Judy's house and wanted her to come out and play, I'd SING, *"Juudeee,"* in a sing-songy voice. She'd sing, *"Elllaa,"* when she wanted me to play. It was truly a unique thing about Baumann Street. No other kids I knew ever sang for their playmates.

Judy's brother Wally was two weeks older than I, and he had a crush on me when we were 5. He said he was going to marry me and we'd move to Texas where he would protect me from tornadoes. He kissed me a couple of times in his garage.

My older brother Jimmy was born a blue baby, that is, he had hemophilia. It was not unusual for my parents to rush him to the hospital for the slightest injury. I'm convinced that, when I was born, they probably were terrified that I, too, might have the disease. Luckily, I was healthy. Jimmy and I often got into trouble together, since we were close in age. Mom used to chase us with a broom (so not to hurt Jimmy) when she was angry, but one time he ran upstairs to the second story of our 4-square, brown-and-white house, and out to the back porch, climbed over the railing, slid down the small roof, grabbed the clothesline, and jumped to the ground, uninjured. My mother almost had a heart attack. After that, she had one of those paddle-ball toys to spank me. Dad had his belt. Jimmy remained unscathed. However, one summer day, neighbor Mrs. Bielinski reported to my mom that Jimmy was peeing off the back porch. Mom lectured him. Boys will be boys, I guess. But I wasn't too happy when he peed down the chimney of my metal doll house. And once, on vacation at Honeoye Lake, he peed through a knothole in the second floor of the cottage and it went straight into Grandpa Littlebetter's slipper. It was a big surprise for Grandpa that morning.

Dad signed up Jimmy and me to appear on *Uncle Eddie's Clubhouse* on WHEC, Channel 10, in 1954.

*Jimmy and Me
with Eddie Meath*

Eddie Meath talked to each kid in the "peanut gallery." He asked me if I had a joke. I had prepared one, but was too shy to say it on camera. We have pictures from our TV set.

Marcia told me the story about the day that Jimmy was sent out of his OLPH class and into the school's hallway for misbehaving, but had disappeared when his teacher checked on him. The nuns were frantically looking for him because of his illness. They got Marcia out of class to help. As Marcia passed the stairway where all the chocolate "chill" was crated for morning break, she heard, "Pssst, Marcia!" There was Jimmy hiding under the stairs!

Marcia pulled a stunt like that, too. She didn't want to go to First Communion practice because the kids from No. 22 School would beat up the OLPH kids, so she hid in the tall grass of a vacant lot on Baumann Hill with a pack of cough drops (to eat) and her Mickey Mouse watch to know when it was time to go home for lunch. Unfortunately for her, Grandma Fedyk came walking by looking for dandelion greens and saw her. "Marcia! What are you doing in the grass?" she asked in broken English. She led Marcia home before she could even respond. Mom wrote up some excuse for her absence then drove her to school where she had to participate in her First Communion practice.

Before starting kindergarten, I had to have a polio shot and whatever other ones were required by law. Mom took me to the OLPH kindergarten room on Joseph Avenue to wait in line for the nurse. When the nurse got to me, she saw my name was Eloise and felt it necessary to say something cute. "Oh, your name is Eloise! Are you like the Eloise on TV?" (*Eloise at the Plaza*, etc.) I snarled, kicked her in the shin, and screamed, "No!" I bet she was sorry she asked.

I was assigned to a red-and-white table for four in kindergarten. I got to meet all my classmates for the first time, most of whom stayed with my class for nine years. Unfortunately, the teacher sat me with Freddy B., a nice kid, but he had a lisp. After getting spit in my face the first day, I insisted that Sr. Dolores Theresa move me to a different table. I wasn't going to put up with *that* for eight months.

The dreamboat of our class was Corky P., who was tall with curly blonde hair. Every girl in our kindergarten through 8th Grade class had a crush on him. To my utter disappointment, he never spoke to me in nine years, but I did dance with him at my Aunt Joanne's wedding when I was 7 years old. (His sister was my Aunt Joanne's maid-of-honor and I was Joanne's flower girl.) The dance was unforgettable for me. (I am now friends with Corky on Facebook. How things change!)

Since we had to walk home from school at lunch time (and walk back), I often ate lunch at Grandma Littlebetter's since she was only two blocks from school. She always had French toast, freshly made banana bread, cherry or strawberry Jell-O with fruit, and the most delicious devil's food cake with confectionary sugar frosting. To die for!

We often visited Grandma and Grandpa because they didn't have a car, and Grandma was quite heavy and it was difficult for her to walk up Baumann Hill to our house, although she did visit when she was younger (50s & 60s). One day she cleaned my bedroom and, when I got home from school, I almost fainted—she threw away all my broken crayons, which I used for "shading." I was devastated, but I forgave her. Eventually.

Littlebetter (Malolepszy) Family

She always had coloring books and crayons at her house to keep us kids busy and we loved them. She also had a wide-arm rocking chair in her "hall," where she sang lots of Polish songs to my cousin Bonnie and me, as we each sat on an arm of the chair. I thought "Frere Jacques" was Polish, too. (How would I know the difference?) A nursery rhyme she sang to me was, *"There once was a girl, who had a little curl, right in the middle of her forehead. When she was good, she was very, very good, and when she was bad, she was horrid."* Hmmm.

Grandpa was born in Middleport, NY, and was an upholsterer (with his brother Bill) and walked to work every day. A signature feature of his work was all the hammered brass nail heads holding the upholstery in place. Grandma was born in Buffalo, NY, but her family moved to Albion, NY. She told us the story that she once had a job as a waitress in Point Breeze where a customer offered to take her and a couple of other girls for a ride in his boat. The boat was overloaded, water was lapping at the top of the boat, and it almost sank! She was terrified because she couldn't swim.

My grandparents were very poor but my mother always made sure they had groceries. My Uncle Johnny always mowed their lawn and shoveled their snow. Grandma had her own wringer wash machine, which I found fascinating. I tried it a few times with her supervision.

Mom's younger sister Joanne and her very handsome new husband John Wroblewski had an apartment over Otto's Tavern on Remington Street. Johnny was part owner and helped Otto with bartending and preparing fish fries (yum). Joanne and Johnny had a baby daughter Carol, and sometimes Marcia would babysit and I'd go with her. We'd read comic books and watch TV while tending to the baby and get to eat a free fish fry.

One school day, Mom told me to walk to Joanne's for lunch and meet her there, but when I got there, the outside door was locked and there was no bell. I screamed for Mom, banged on the door, and cried. I thought I might have been mistaken about her instructions, so I ran all the way home, but no one was there and the house was locked tight. I thought my mother abandoned me. Standing at the corner of Laser Street by Jake's Deli, I cried and cried, and then went back to school without any lunch. She asked later why I never came. I was angry and hurt and told her what happened. She felt badly because they never heard me pounding on the door.

11

Johnny and Joanne had a small cottage in the Times-Union Tract of Honeoye Lake and we would stay with them for a day or sometimes a week. We'd go swimming (Marcia's favorite pastime), play songs on a real jukebox (no money needed!) like "You Are My Sunshine," "Zulu Warrior," and "Let Me Go, Lover," and use their stinky chemical toilet. (I didn't like that much.) Johnny had to take his trash to the dump once a week, and one Saturday when I was about 5, I asked, "Uncle Johnny, can I go to the dump with you?" Everybody laughed, but I enjoyed the adventure, and I had a crush on Johnny and got to ride "shotgun" in his car.

On another day, Marcia and I walked up the Times-Union Tract hill to Specksgoor's general store on East Lake Road where I saw a little baby doll wearing a white dress with tiny blue flowers that I just had to have. When Dad gave me money to go back and buy it because I was "Daddy's little girl," it was one of my happiest memories of my childhood!

Mom's older sister, Regina (Jean) and her husband Herb Godon had two daughters, Bonnie (a year younger than me) and Gayle (a few years younger). They moved to Irondequoit, NY, when I was small. One night, when I slept over at Bonnie's, Gayle climbed into our bed, sat on my head and farted. I couldn't escape. She still laughs about it to this day. Herb worked at Kodak but also played the drums in a band. Sometimes little Bonnie and Gayle would sing "Sandman" along with the band—a real crowd pleaser!

Uncle Richard (Mom's younger brother) and his wife Lillian had three children, Cheryl, Ricky, and Chris Little (they shortened their last name). Ricky looked like Ricky Nelson—

so handsome! Uncle Richard and Ricky are living together as I write this.

While the family was ever-changing, Grandma and Grandpa Littlebetter continued to enjoy the view from their "hall" overlooking the sidewalk on VanStallen Street when the weather was poor, but they really loved sitting on their front porch in the summer. It was their social life. Grandma would wave to everyone in hopes they would stop to chat. They were one of three next-door neighbors who made Ripley's Believe It or Not list: Good, Littlebetter, and Best. In later years, a black family moved across the road and their son's name was "Wendell." Grandma assumed they said "Window," and thought it was a very "comical" name. Oh, Grandma!

Speaking of comical, Grandma's favorite TV show was *Benny Hill* because it made her laugh so much. Grandpa loved watching baseball, both on TV and at Red Wing Stadium on Norton Street, which was only three blocks away from his house. Grandpa always swore at the players; they never did anything right.

Although Grandma was my rock, she was a worry-wart like me. Once, relatives from Poland were staying with them and the men were passed out drunk on the floor and she had to step over them to cook dinner. Feeling anxious, she went to see a doctor and was prescribed some medicine. When the next appointment came around, she took the bus downtown and found the entire building was gone. She resigned to dealing with it herself.

Church was extremely important in our family, and Mom, Grandma, and I would often go to the OLPH novenas to the Blessed Mother on Tuesday nights. The sound of the heavenly voices in the softly lit church singing "Oh, Mary, My Mother" moved me to tears. (Yes, I really had a heart.) One winter, Mom picked up Grandma for church on Sunday morning, but it was icy and Grandma fell and slipped right under our Chevy! Getting her out was another matter. It took all of us.

Grandma, Mom, Marcia, and I frequently saw movies at the Sun Theater on the corner of Joseph Avenue and Weyl Street on Saturday afternoons. My most memorable movie was *House of Wax*, with Vincent Price. Even though I was 5 years old, the possible death of the (naked!) girl in the last scenes affected me greatly.

Judy and Wally Gekoski used to go the Sun Theater with me, as well. After seeing *The Blob* in 1958, I was afraid to sleep alone, so I slept at Judy's. Wally kept coming in the bedroom teasing that the Blob was coming through our heating vent. He also had to share a dirty joke, which he thought was funny. Something about "rubber balls and liquor." He was just showing off.

Grandma was 92 when she passed away, not from having a mastectomy in her late 80s, not from her strokes, but just happiness to be with Grandpa again at the same nursing home. She died a few days after arriving there. Grandpa Littlebetter was a long-time smoker, but despite colon and oral cancers, he lived to be 99 years old.

Dad and His Family

MY OTHER GRANDPARENTS, Michael and Mary Fedyk, lived on Weyl Street near the foot of Baumann Hill, which meant they also had to climb it when they came to see us. But everybody WALKED back then; nobody drove a car unless they HAD to.

I wasn't especially close to my paternal grandparents. Grandma didn't speak English very well, but she was very tiny and very sweet. She called me "The 'lilla' one" (little one). She had two parakeets at two different times, both named "Tommy." Grandpa always offered me a Coca-Cola®. As a child, I was fascinated by their very old house with an ancient wood smell. (It probably was a fire trap.) They had two stories but they lived on the first floor, with the bathroom (with a pull-chain toilet) out in the main hallway. Two bedrooms had a connecting closet, which we kids would hide in. The ceilings were tin. Their "grandmother's clock" came with Grandpa from Austria. (Luckily, Dad was fixing it at the time of the house sale or we'd never have it.) Their coffee tables were blue glass. And they painted their own Ukrainian Easter Eggs. Once, Grandpa painted them without draining them first. Pew. That wasn't a good idea.

Dad's uncle, Peter Fedyk, lived upstairs in the house on Weyl Street, sharing the same bathroom in the downstairs hallway. He had married the mayor's daughter in Poland. When Pete was going to be conscripted for the Polish army, he came to the U.S., but his wife refused to follow him here. He lived alone until he died at age 79 in a fall down the stairs, drunk.

The Fedyks did have an interesting history.

Grandma Fedyk (Mary Szczech) was born in Poland around 1886. She was one of nine children. Her mother, also named Mary, married Great Grandpa Martin Szczech, who was a coffin maker, and when he died, she remarried and had a son John. Grandma's other brothers were Stanley (Stanislaw) Szczech, who was a tailor and a watch repairer, and Joe Szczech, who was also a tailor and a bartender. A third brother was a violinist in Poland and performed for weddings and bar mitzvahs. After one performance he walked across an ice-covered pond and fell in, but he didn't drown. However, he died a few days later of pneumonia.

Grandma's mother worked in a Jewish bakery and hid Jewish people in her home.

Grandma came to the U.S. through Ellis Island with her brother Stanley (1908), and Joe followed, but she was lonely and went back to Poland. Living conditions in Poland were even worse than before, so she came back to the U.S., departing from Bremen, Germany. I heard two stories of her voyages: The first ship's captain loved her long brown hair that touched her heels, and allowed her to travel first class. She was on the second boat with Mr. Foreman (Rochester store magnate), who fell in love with Grandma and tried to kiss her onboard. Ooo.

Grandpa Fedyk lived in Galicia, Austria, with his family, but considered himself Ukrainian. (The land boundaries changed all the time back then!) He immigrated to the U.S. around 1908 and lived in Brooklyn, where he met Grandma. Then both families decided to settle in Rochester. He had three brothers: Peter, Andrew, and Dimitri (called Dan). Peter (the same Peter who lived on Weyl Street) was a dancer in the Russian Ballet Troupe and became a chef at Highland Hospital in Rochester. Dan was an upholsterer. Andrew had a tailor shop on Joseph Avenue directly across from Laser Street (off Baumann). One day Grandpa Fedyk bought a Ford Model-T and crashed it right into the tailor shop because he didn't know how to brake. End of story. And the car. He never drove again.

Grandma and Grandpa married in St. Stanislaus church when Grandma was about 17. For a time, Grandma Fedyk worked in a thread factory. (She was also an unwilling medium and saw ghosts at least twice.) Grandpa Fedyk worked at the Eggleston Hotel (after hours; i.e., a "speakeasy") and then at Kodak in the Roll Paper Division. They had four children, James Myron (Dad), Benjamin (Mitch), Helen, and another son, Walter, who died of diphtheria at age 2.

My dad was a "prankster," and almost killed his mother with his science experiment in the bathroom, mixing bleach with ammonia. He also taunted her with a fake rat and she fainted. He did the same thing with my little black fur-edged boot—threw it at my mom and said it was a bird from the basement. He laughed while she screamed. Bad! When Charles Lindbergh landed his plane in Rochester, Dad was there, ran out to the runway, and got knocked down by the plane, or so he said.

Fedyk Family

On occasion, Dad borrowed films from Kodak to show on a projector. Often, they were cartoons or *The Three Stooges*. However, one time he brought home a documentary on Bali, showing bare-breasted women. I was shocked, left the room, and was sure he was going to hell. Grandpa Littlebetter asked him to show it again. They were both going to hell!

Dad believed Rochester to be "his" city. He loved it like no one else I know. He knew the history and he shared it with us, not just with words, but taking us to places children rarely went, showing us brick roads, old train stations (and a story of how he used to smell bear grease in the torn-down one), historical buildings, and going on the last-ever Rochester Subway ride. (We have home movies.) We picked (and ate) mushrooms from the parks in the fall. He took us to the Children's Pavilion in Highland Park where we ran like "wild Indians" up and down the stairs. We sometimes went to Front Street to see all the poultry shops (live chickens), meat markets (dead pigs), bars, tobacco and liquor stores, and various sundry shops—and all the people milling about. The backs of the 5-or-more-story decrepit buildings were dangling over the Genesee River, with clotheslines on back porches and bedding hanging out the windows. I wondered how those people dared to live there. It terrified me. He also told us stories about the "great curiosity" of Rattlesnake Pete and his "museum," with numerous snakes and potions to cure blood-poisoning, boils, and even "felons!"

Dad believed that the Fedyk name would be famous one day. When FedEx was named, it sort of fit the bill. Fedyks/FedEx. Get it? Pronounced the same. Haha. (I tried.)

Dad was an outdoorsy guy. He absolutely loved fishing. In all of our vacation photos, there were always several pictures of strings of fish that Dad caught. His fishing buddies, John Ptaszek and Bob Willer, both from the Kodak Hawkeye Plant, were in many shots. John used to call me "heart face," so he was a favorite of mine! John eventually moved to California and started a photofinishing business, I believe, and offered Dad a job. After we kids complained about leaving our friends, he decided not to go. I'm sure he had other reasons for not going, as well, but he was disappointed. It could have made him rich—or richer than we already were.

Dad

During Rochester's race riots, Dad had to take our next-door neighbor Mrs. Milbredt to St. Mary's Hospital due to an injury with her lawn mower. He had to drive down Joseph Avenue with people climbing on his car and hitting the windows with baseball bats! He got through the frenzy and safely got Mrs. Milbredt to the ER, but drove home a different way.

For Mother's Day, we always got Mom a basket of pansies with different-colored faces. She always planted them along the driveway by the side door, along with her gladiolas. Dad's pride and joy were his roses in the backyard. We had a Blaze climbing rose bush that served as a backdrop for all our graduation pictures, and he had hybrid tea roses, like John F. Kennedy, Peace, Masquerade, and Tropicana. When I was small, we'd go to the Jackson & Perkins Rose Garden in Newark, NY, in June to see all the varieties and smell the lovely scent of each rose. It was glorious!

We often went places with the Swajkos family—Carl, Rosemary, Linda (Lala), and Elaine. Elaine and I were close in age and shared a love of playing paper dolls and, in our teenage years, we were ardent fans of George Maharis. Mom went to grammar school with Rosemary's sister Marion, who died young (40?), but Mom was also close to Rosemary, who lived with her family on the second floor of a house on Norton Street. And Carl became Dad's good drinking buddy. So they partied together a lot, mostly at our house. But one night when I was about 6, while my family visited them on Norton Street, I asked if I could stay overnight with Elaine, and I did. Her dad came in to say goodnight and to turn off the lights, and clearly warned us, "No monkeyshines!" Well, I couldn't stop laughing because I never heard that phrase before. I think I laughed all night. (They never invited me back, to that house, at least.) The next day was a Saturday and we were up to no good. There was a family across the street who Elaine and Linda thought were "bad," and Elaine wanted to get back at them for something. I didn't know who they were or what Elaine was up to. She cleverly showed me how to wrap up dog poop in paper and set it on fire, which she did on their sidewalk! She rang their doorbell and they came out and stomped on the fire. Well, you can imagine what happened next. We ran away like bats out of hell! (If Dad ever found out, I would have gotten "the belt.")

Speaking of playing paper dolls (we called them "cut-outs"), I had boxes of them and sometimes I'd spread them out in the dining room (which was rarely used except for playing piano). Dad told me to pick them up, but I was typically obstinate and didn't do it because I was still playing. The next day they were in a burn barrel in the backyard! I saw embers of Katy Keene, Elizabeth Taylor, and Betty Grable paper gowns and furs floating out from the fire. I seethed for days, weeks, months, years. How could he destroy something he knew I loved so much? (Thank goodness my favorite set was still in a box in my room.) I know it was my fault for not listening, but I wasn't "Daddy's little girl" after that. I don't think we were on speaking terms for years, until my next rebellion, which only made things worse between us. *Sigh*.

Life In the 1950s

LIFE WAS SO DIFFERENT when I was a little kid in Rochester, NY, in the early 1950s. It was home to three corporate giants—Bausch & Lomb, Eastman Kodak Company, and Xerox Corporation. Jobs were plentiful, and employers fully covered your health care! Not so much any more. Now, the largest employers are the University of Rochester, Rochester Regional Health, and Wegmans and there aren't as many job opportunities.

Rochester still boasts three beautiful waterfalls within city limits, and various cultural centers and museums. It's still a great place to live. But the 50s? They were special. It was a time of transition from "war" to "peace." A time when ethnic groups lived side by side, opening businesses, sharing their ideas, culture, music, and food. A time of expansion into the suburbs and homebuilding. A time to say goodbye to old technologies and accept new ones, like television and automatic washers and dryers. And a time of nuclear power and the beginning of space travel with Sputnik. The baby boomers—that is, the babies born after World War II—were the children of change. We saw it every day in our own lives.

As I've said, I grew up on Baumann Street, off Ave D, between Hudson and Joseph Avenues. It was a relatively new neighborhood then, with some vacant lots and houses being built. Now it's an impoverished neighborhood. Our house was a typical "four-square," two-story home. It had a front porch by the front door where you could socialize with your friends and neighbors, a side door (which we called the "cellar door"), three bedrooms, and one full bathroom.

46 Baumann Street

At that time, we had a coal bin and a monster coal furnace in the basement. The coal man came every winter, opened the window to the coal bin, put his chute in the window, and pulled a lever to release the coal into the bin. Dad would shovel the coal into the furnace to keep the fire going 24 hours a day during the winter, and the furnace had huge arms going to all the rooms in the house. We used to call the coal bin the "dungeon," and we'd sometimes play in there and get filthy. The coal was great to draw with on the sidewalk! Dad also had his work bench in the cellar and it always smelled like sawdust down there.

An ice man delivered huge chunks of ice to our next-door neighbor, Miss Wilson, who had no electricity in her old farmhouse. (She did have gas lighting.) The ice man would give me small chunks of ice to suck on in the summer. We also had a "rag man" who collected old clothes, a guy on a bicycle who sharpened scissors, and a kiddie ride (the Dipsy Doodle) pulled by a truck through the neighborhood in the summer.

At the corner of our street, where Baumann met Avenue D, there was Charlie's bar on one corner and Esther's grocery store on the other. Mom had an account with Esther's and every transaction was recorded in a "book," which had a white top sheet for Esther and a yellow copy for Mom. They would reconcile the book at the end of every month and Mom would pay off her account. If I paid in cash, Esther would always make me figure out the change. My eyes would glass over and I'd look at her like she was an alien. I found the big "grippers" to grab the cereal boxes on the top shelf fascinating, and I loved the 1¢ candy and 5¢ Popsicles, Fudgsicles, and Creamsicles. Yum! For big grocery shopping, Mom drove to Star Market on Joseph Avenue and Avenue D.

My younger sister Patty walked by Esther's one morning and saw her girlfriend Patty Logel (whose dad owned Charlie's) standing at the counter. My sister went to surprise her by jumping on her back, with her arms around her neck and her legs around her waist. Uh, except that it wasn't Patty

Logel. It was a little, old Polish lady!! I bet that was a shock for both of them!

Back to our house... On the first floor of our house, we had a small kitchen that Dad remodeled with green tile when I was still a toddler. He built a pantry and broom closet across from the cellar door. The kitchen had a set of windows looking out into the backyard so Mom could sit at the table, play Solitaire, drink her coffee or Genny beer, smoke her Salem cigarette, watch Dialing for Dollars on a small TV on a rickety stand, and "supervise" our play outside, not that she really did. Next to the refrigerator, there was a heat register where we used to stand and get warm on a cold winter day. Mom washed our hair in the kitchen sink every Saturday night and set it in rollers. She did this for me until I got a job and I started washing my own hair in the shower every day. (She thought I was crazy to shower every day! It was a waste of water and bad for my skin. Plus, Dad didn't want to clean hair out of the tub drain.) We (I) took in some stray cats, on occasion, much to Mom's chagrin. No one took animals to the vet; they just came and went as they pleased. Packs of wild dogs used to roam the streets, terrifying me when I walked to school.

In the early 50s, we had a dining room with a piano and a Victrola. Later the Victrola was replaced by our first Hi-Fi— a Webcor record player for 45s and 33-1/3 LPs. I still loved listening to the old 78 rpm records, though, like "Hey, Doc," "I Don't Want to Set the World on Fire," and "Three Little Fishies." I remember having a pet turtle in a dish with a ramp that was placed on the unused Victrola, and we had a couple of parakeets (Marilyn and Mickey). Marilyn wouldn't leave the mirror and the poop piled up in one spot.

Later, in the 60s, Dad painted a scene of Honeoye Lake (on a soffit above the upright piano) that we revered for many years. Eventually, Dad took an axe to our piano. We were all horrified, but he was tired of seeing our "stuff" piled on the top. The painting remained and Patty has it today. Dad remodeled the dining room, bought a blonde dining room set, and made built-in cabinets (covered in Formica) for Mom's china, plus a desk for the phone, and a row of drawers for tablecloths and "treasured things" that were only used on special occasions.

The living room had 40s-style furniture when I was little, but after Jimmy died in 1955, Dad bought a stylish, silk lilac sectional couch and a gray wool carpet with a lovely swirl design, blonde side tables and coffee table, modern lamps, and starburst clocks. The "nuclear" age had begun, complete with "atomic" design. It looked like it came out of *Better Homes and Gardens!* Dad always had to have the latest and the best.

I can still hear the stairs creak as we climbed them to the second floor, and the squeaking of Mom's wicker laundry basket, which she carried up and down the stairs almost every day. I can also hear the rattle of the leaded-glass door going to the front entry.

Originally, we had an open porch, but when I was 12, I was sitting out there with my friend Elaine Swajkos until her family left around midnight. A few minutes later, when I was in bed, there was a loud crash that shook the house. A strange man came running up our stairs and grabbed me and yelled to everyone to get out, fast. There was a car that had crashed into our porch, and the engine was smoking. Two teens ran away from the accident. If Elaine and I had still been sitting there, we would have died. With the insurance, Dad contracted builders to enclose the porch, but it was never the same social experience as we used to have, watching the people go by.

On the second story of the house, Jimmy's bedroom and my parents' bedroom overlooked the roof of the front porch. Sometimes we kids would climb out there just for fun. Mom was never happy about that. Jimmy's closet had a step in it, and I was convinced that it housed some treasure. Sometimes I hid in there and Mom would have to find me. I remember the cowboy bedspread on Jimmy's bed and the linoleum flooring. In later years, it became Mickey's bedroom and, for a while, Patty's crib was in there as well.

Mom and Dad had a very scratchy brown woolen blanket that they used for over forty years on a mattress they never replaced. Dad had a blonde armoire for his suits (including an old zoot suit!), and Mom had a matching dresser, with one drawer dedicated to all her jewelry. She used to have a vanity with a bench seat and large, round mirror, which was later hung in the dining room when Dad remodeled it. Mom and Dad had a silver and black "dresser set" (brush, comb, powder jar, nail files, etc.) that was displayed on top of the dresser on a doily. Mom also had a fancy jewelry box.

Marcia and I shared a bedroom, then for a while it was just mine, then Patty's and mine. Dad bought me and Marcia twin beds and a new ash-blonde dresser. One side was Marcia's and the other side was mine, although I always snooped on her side and used her perfumes. The confetti linoleum was eventually replaced by hardwood floors, which Patty and I scratched up in no time.

Across from our bedroom was a walk-in closet. There were decals all over the walls—Little Bo Peep, sheep, and other characters. Next to the closet was the only bathroom. Before Dad remodeled, there were decals on the bathroom walls, too—I particularly remember the "Squirt" character from Squirt soda (which we called "pop"). In the late 50s, Dad installed baby blue bath fixtures and added a storage cabinet in the corner so Mom could stack her crossword-puzzle books and he could read the latest copy of *Field & Stream.*

Next to the bathroom was a door to the back porch. The railing was never sturdy and Dad didn't want us playing out there but it was a great place to oversee the entire block.

Across from my parents' bedroom was the attic door, which never stayed shut unless you turned the skeleton key. The stairs creaked with every step. The attic was full of old books, bins of fine china and glass, clothes on a rack, a storage locker or two, and many, many toys. We often used it as a play room. Mickey and Patty used to smoke up there until we caught them. Some of the floorboards were loose and I used to hide things under them, like jewelry. Once I didn't like the coconut Easter egg I received and hid it under the floorboard. It's probably still there.

Not everyone had a car, but my dad did. In fact, not everyone had a garage or even a driveway! The first car I remember was Dad's 1950 Chevy 2 coupe. As kids, we knew every car make and model—there weren't very many. On summer afternoons my girlfriend Judy and I would play "cars" while we sat on the porch steps. I'd say, "The first car is mine!" We'd laugh if it was a junker. The next car would be Judy's. We'd ooh and aah if it was a sporty new one.

My mom could drive, too, at a time when most women never learned how and relied on their husbands to chauffeur them around. Many husbands did not believe that women should drive, and almost all households only had one car. Mothers stayed at home to raise the children, and usually did not have jobs, except perhaps at Sibley's or Kodak. In those days, you had to go to each store to pay your bill or put money down for your lay-away. Mom always kept track of every penny spent.

During the school year, Mom would sometimes drive us back to school after lunch, if she had errands to run. One summer, she was supposed to pick up Dad's check but she pulled into the school parking lot instead. When I asked her why she was there, she just said, "Oh! The horse knows the way!"

We also had a black, desk model, rotary-dial telephone with a "party line." You could pick up the phone and hear someone's conversation. You respected their privacy and waited till they were done to make your call, unless there was an emergency, in which case, you'd interrupt the conversation and ask if you could make the call. My dad hated the telephone; the only reason he permitted it was to call for an ambulance. We didn't have 911 then. We had "exchanges" and numbers like HOpkins 7-2786. Eventually it was updated to all numbers—467-2786, and it was years before we were assigned an Area Code.

Dad always threatened to tear the phone out of the wall (he might have done that once or twice). He found it very intrusive and a waste of time to chat with people you saw all the time. If the phone rang and if he answered it, he'd say, "Joe's Bar and Grill" or some other silly thing. One time,

Sister Marie Therese from Nazareth Academy called, and when Dad answered, he said, "City Morgue." She hung up quickly. Dad laughed his butt off. When she called back again, I answered. Who was the adult?

One evening Dad did have to use the phone for an emergency. I had gone across the street to Judy Gekoski's house to do my homework with her. There was a thunderstorm and it seemed to be right above us. I was sitting at her dining room table, looking out at my house, when I saw a bolt of lightning hit my house and travel down a wire on the outside (by the cellar door), running from the top of the house and into the ground with a big "flash!" I gasped and, as soon as it was safe, I ran home. Firetrucks arrived and the firemen found that the lightning burned a hole in the roof (about a foot in diameter), hitting a wire encased in an iron pipe in the attic, then traveling into the ground, as I witnessed.

Our television was everything. When I was a toddler, I remember looking behind the TV set to see how everyone got inside. It was mind blowing! *The Ed Sullivan Show. The Life of Riley. Tom Corbett, Space Cadet. Roy Rogers. The Lone Ranger. Rootie Kazootie. Your Show of Shows with Sid Caesar. I Remember Mama. My Little Margie. Red Skelton.* The list of shows we watched together as a family was endless. And the ads were interesting and fun to watch as well, from Halo Shampoo to Bardahl Motor Oil, from 20-Mule-Team Borax to Dinah Shore singing, *"See the USA in your Chevrolet."* It was a great time to be alive.

The Day My Parents Cried

ON MY SEVENTH birthday (April 16, 1955), I received a blue two-wheeler bicycle. I was so excited that I could now ride a bike to the "Fedyk family playground" on Wakefield Street near Hudson Avenue, which today is the Keeler Street Expressway. Marcia, our next-door friend Rozzie Milbredt, my brother Jimmy, and I went there a few times on our bikes. My bike was in better shape than Jimmy's so it wasn't unusual for him to ask me if he could ride my bike around the block or to the playground. I always said yes, but I would follow him, walking.

On Saturday, May 21, 1955, Jimmy asked to borrow my bike for a spin around the block. He headed for Fairbanks Street and I followed. He was a few houses down, in the road, when some boy called out his name and mocked him for riding a girl's bike. Jimmy turned around to see who was talking, and rammed into an old, gray Studebaker parked at the curb. He fell off my bike and hit his head on the curb. He stood up, crying. I was terrified, because I knew he'd have to get to the hospital. I walked the bike back home as he walked on his own. Mom and Dad immediately took him to Northside Hospital on Portland Avenue. It looked bad.

Jimmy was holding his head with his hands and screaming in pain.

I started walking around the block, looking for the boy who made fun of Jimmy. I wanted to beat him up, and I would have, if I had found him. I circled the entire block, going down Fairbanks to Hudson to Dayton and back to Baumann. But he was gone and I didn't know where he lived.

My parents didn't come home that night. Marcia and I went to Grandma Littlebetter's where my aunts and uncles sat with us, very somber. My Aunt Jean tried to make me feel better by saying that, if they come home with Jimmy, everything will be okay. The truth was, he had to have surgery—there was blood on his brain, the worst thing that could happen to a hemophiliac. She didn't think I'd understand, but I fully understood.

The next morning, May 22, when Mom and Dad pulled up to the curb, Jimmy was not with them (not that I expected him to be). Jimmy had died in surgery. They were crying softly at first, but then sobbing as they sat with us in Grandma's living room, surrounded by large, framed pictures of Jesus and Mary with rays of grace coming from their hearts and hands.

I went up to Mom, hugged her and said, "Mommy, it'll be okay. Jesus will watch over Jimmy." At that point, she wailed and hugged me hard. I felt so helpless. And I knew my brother, my playmate, was gone forever. I knew, because my teacher prepared my class and particularly me and another classmate, for death. There was a boy in my class with a disease, and it was her way of assuring that we wouldn't be confused or traumatized as much if we knew that people went to heaven to be with Jesus when they died. It did help me to cope, for sure.

My new two-wheeler bike went in the attic, never to see the light of day again. I knew better than to question it.

Jimmy was laid out in his Cub Scout uniform at the Funk Funeral Home next to the OLPH convent. Everyone was crying. The Knights of St. John came in and saluted Jimmy with their swords and everyone said the rosary. I went up to Jimmy to peek under his Cub Scout cap; he was bald.

The hardest part occurred the morning of the burial. I walked by my parents' bedroom and saw Dad sitting on the bed in his boxer shorts, crying his heart out. It was heartbreaking. There was nothing I could do, so I just went back to the bedroom I shared with Marcia to think about everything that had just happened. I let Jimmy ride my bike. I never found that boy who caused all this to happen. I wanted to beat his lights out but was unable. I was taking some of the blame on myself for Jimmy's death. But I knew he was sick before I was born, and there wasn't anything I could do about that.

Jimmy lies near the railroad tracks in Holy Sepulchre Cemetery. At least he can hear the trains go by, as he waits patiently in heaven for the rest of us to come.

Stranger Danger

"IT WAS A DARK NIGHT IN THE CITY," explains Guy Noir from the *Prairie Home Companion* radio program. For a small city, Rochester had its share of major crimes—mob hits, heists, serial killings, bombings, riots, rapes, illegal drug transactions, and everyday shootings. But there were sinister things going on that were rarely talked about, especially by children.

When I was in grammar school, I walked the half mile to school in the morning, walked home for lunch then back to school, and walked home again at the end of the day. It was challenging at times—in intense heat, during snowstorms, and when I wasn't feeling well. I had other challenges as well—perverts.

They were out there. I knew I shouldn't ever speak to strangers, but, in 1958 when I was in 4th grade, it was my usual routine to walk back to school after lunch via Grandma Littlebetter's street. It felt safe and familiar and many kids in my class lived there. On this particular day, I was a block away from school when a 1951 mist-green Chevy coupe pulled alongside of me. A man about my father's age, with dark hair, asked if I knew how to get to some street I didn't hear. I was very suspicious, but I inched a little closer to hear the name of the street. What I saw through the window stopped me in my tracks. He had his penis in his hand. One look at that and I went running to school as fast as my legs would carry me.

We always had to stand in line outside of school until the doors opened. My classmate "J." was in front of me and I told her about the incident and how scared I was. She asked if I would like a ride home with her dad. I agreed without hesitation. At 3 p.m., I walked out to her dad's car. It was a 1951 mist-green Chevy coupe! Terrified, I stood there like stone; I didn't know what to do. Her father fit the same description of the man I saw. "J." hopped into the car and sat in the middle of the bench seat. She said, "Come on. My dad will take you home." I got in, hugging the door all the way. I prayed it wasn't the same guy, but I never knew for sure. But "J."'s father knew where I lived.

During the winter in 8th grade, I was on my way home from church on a snowy Sunday morning, wearing a long, red coat. I was about to turn from Weaver Street onto Baumann Street when a teenage guy pulled alongside of me and cried in a mocking voice, "Where are you going, Little Red Riding Hood?" Then he stuck out his tongue and licked around his mouth in a sensual way. I started running, but I had a long way to go, including up Baumann Hill in the snow! He didn't pursue me all the way, but enjoyed taunting me for a few more minutes.

Perhaps the most frightening time happened on a Saturday. I decided to attend 8 a.m. Mass (something I enjoyed doing on occasion). After Mass, I was at the base of Baumann Hill when a guy in his 20s pulled alongside of me, telling me to get in his car. I sensed this to be an extremely dangerous situation. I kept walking briskly, but he easily kept pace. Another car turned the corner and forced him to move along, or go around the block, which he appeared to do as he turned on Laser Street at the top of Baumann Hill. I took that opportunity to run home as fast as I could. My mother was in the kitchen when I stormed in breathlessly, screaming that some guy was chasing me. I ran to the front door and saw him drive by a few times, checking out yards and porches. I was shaking like a leaf. My mother didn't take it seriously, though, which dismayed me. She tsk-tsk'd and that was it! I don't know if she didn't believe me, or was clueless what to do. Or maybe she was preoccupied by Dialing for Dollars. Yeah, that probably was it.

After that, I was on the alert for perverts. Riding the city bus to high school and, later, my job, brought me in contact with some of them. There was a really, really old, disgusting man who waited at my Hudson Avenue bus stop every day and would insist that I get on first—so he could pinch my butt. I reported him to the bus driver, who shrugged and did nothing. Marcia said the same nasty old guy used to do the same thing to her! There were other guys on the bus who would "cop a feel" when the bus was packed like sardines. And there were guys who drove by the bus stop every day and tried to pick me up, but that's a later story.

A Changing Family

I DISTINCTLY REMEMBER when I found out Mom was pregnant. We were visiting Marion and Ben Armes in Webster and their family— Nancy, Norma, and Kenny—on the hill above the Irondequoit Bay. Once in a while, I would stay overnight with Nancy, who was my age, and my parents would pick me up the next day. On this occasion, Mr. Armes taught me how to shoot at tin cans with his rifle, as his kids were already good at it. (Mom would have had a heart attack to see me with a gun.)

Norma said to me in a teasing way, "Your mother's going to have a baby. Nyah, nyah."

I was in denial. I replied, "No, she isn't! She's just getting fat!"

Norma challenged me to ask her, which I did when she arrived to pick me up. She said, "Of course, I'm having a baby!"

I was CRUSHED. Not because of the baby, or because I would no longer be "their baby," but because they never considered to tell me, and I had to find out through Norma. I was thoroughly embarrassed by my lack of family information.

Michael Lawrence Fedyk was born November 9, 1957, when Mom was 38 years old and I was 9. He was healthy. My parents were elated about having a son again. His crib was put into Jimmy's old room.

The following July, Mom announced that she was pregnant again. An accident. She didn't think she could get pregnant while breast feeding. Oops.

It was that same year when Marcia turned 17 and graduated from Nazareth Academy and decided to join the convent. While my mother was elated at her choice, my dad wasn't so sure. He probably thought she was nuts. At 10 years old, I was glad to have a bedroom to myself—for a while.

Patricia Therese Fedyk was born January 28, 1959, when Mom was almost 40 years old.

Michael (Mickey) went into a twin bed while Patty slept in the crib in his room. They were like two devils from hell, always up to no good, always conniving, always fighting. I had to babysit the times my parents decided to have a night out, going to Charlie's corner bar. It was exhausting. One night I felt the need to spank Mickey for something he did. He laughed, which made me angry. So, when I went to spank him a second time, he looked at me and said, "But, Ella, I love you." I never spanked him again. I felt like a heel.

Eventually, Patty shared my bedroom, but I was getting older and it didn't matter as much to have a play room. I just wanted my books and my radio.

We went to visit Marcia in the convent on special occasions. Once, when she "graduated" to a "novitiate," our entire extended family went to the St. Joseph's Mother House to celebrate out on the lawn. I remember wandering the grounds by myself, looking at all the religious statues. Marcia went on to teach in a number of parishes as Sister Rosarita, including St. Ann, St. Ambrose, Sacred Heart, St. Rose of Lima, St. Mary in Elmira, and St. Francis Xavier on Bay Street.

When Marcia taught at St. Ambrose, the school was set on fire and burned to the ground! And when she was at St. Francis Xavier, a boy in her class threatened to blow up a bomb in her class. No serenity there!

She left the convent, after giving it her best shot for 15 years. She eventually found love with her partner Joe Pino, who was with her for 22 years until he passed away.

A Taste of Humility

AFTER A FUN NIGHT with the Swajkoses at our house, it was time to say goodnight and goodbye. The parents had been drinking while Elaine and I huddled in my room, talking about the new TV show, *Route 66,* and handsome and rugged George Maharis. It was around midnight when we stood at the cellar door as they departed with a few well wishes and "so-longs."

Dad had both hands around my neck. As he talked, I noticed they were getting tighter and tighter around my neck, to the point I couldn't breathe or talk. My tongue was sticking out. I tried to pry off his thick fingers, but he just made them tighter. He was oblivious to my predicament, laughing with Carl as they were getting into the car.

I started to panic.

In a desperate move, I kicked the back of my heel into Dad's shin. It took him by utter surprise. Before I knew it, I was thrown on the kitchen floor and we were pummeling each other with fists, like punching bags. Bam! Bam! Bam! Mom was having a fit, not knowing what the hell was going on and begging us to stop. I told them that he had been choking me. Dad didn't believe a word I said.

I went upstairs crying, leaving them to wonder WTH. I had just been beaten and bruised. Eloise, Famous in Battle, lost her last battle.

Of course, I shouldn't have kicked him. I was just a stupid 12-year-old girl. Did I think it would end well? Probably not, but I thought I could explain my actions. I was so wrong.

I don't think I talked to my father for six years after that, or even got near him. There was a massive rift, and it was a beating I never got over.

Teenage Years

MY TEENAGE YEARS WERE mostly focused on school and music. And, oh yeah, on boys.

I chose to go to Nazareth Academy on Lake Avenue because they did not teach boys. I didn't want the distraction to interfere with my academic work. Really! Honest to God!

Besides, it was comforting to be taught by the Sisters of St. Joseph. Marcia went there before me and sang in the Perosian Choir and appeared on stage wearing beautiful costumes. I was not a good singer (ever) but there were lots of opportunities at Nazareth for lofty goals. I was on the National Honor Society for three years, keeping an above-90 average. I worked on their literary magazine, *Spectrum*, during which time I identified plagiarism by a student and brought it to the attention of our moderator. I was Vice-President of the Future Secretaries Club and arranged all the activities. I was in the English Club, where we acted in after-school skits and put on "teas." And I was in the Latin Club, taking three years of classes. Once, Dad drove me to Canandaigua High School in a blizzard so that I could go to the Latin Convention and have my picture taken in a toga in a chariot! And I hated gym class (except for gymnastics), although I never made an excuse or skipped a class. We had to wear ugly royal blue bloomers and play kickball outside on Lake Ave to be watched by gawking passers-by (gaa), then shower. Thank God we had individual stalls. It was a Catholic school, after all. Modesty above all else.

I loved listening the WBBF 95 in Rochester, with DJs Nick Nickson and Jack Polvino. I voted for my favorite songs. I listened to the Top 40 countdown. I loved Doo-wop, Motown, Dion, the Beatles, and George Maharis. I went to the BBF Prom to see George, and others. I was a typical teenager who hated to leave her bedroom. My books were there, my radio was there; what else is there?

I did share my bedroom with my little sister Patty. I loved her like my own child. She had her bed covered in stuffed animals at all times. Luckily, she was playing with friends most of the time while I was holed up like a hermit.

Then came the boyfriends.

My very first official date was with our soda pop delivery guy, Zygmunt U. at age 16. I wore a blue plaid full skirt with a white blouse, feeling very dressed up to go downtown (on the bus). He took me to see *Lord of the Flies*. God help me. Worst date ever.

That summer, the family went to Honeoye Lake for vacation, staying at Clarence Becherer's cottages (there were four). Our morning newspaper guy called himself Gary Collins, but Collins was his mother's maiden name, I think, and his real last name was Sauerteig. He had a blonde Beatles haircut and was very handsome, indeed. He asked if he could take me on a boat ride and I said sure. He took me to the middle of the lake, stopped the motor, and he kissed me so hard my teeth felt pushed in. Well, (dummy me) went to slap him, but he ducked and I only hit the tip of his nose. But it was my first kiss. Sigh. He drove me back to shore.

The same night, a red-headed, freckle-faced boy named Ray B. from a nearby cottage, sat with me by the campfire and kissed me. Sadly, I wished it had been Gary. Ray and I did become friends, but later he was paralyzed from the neck down in a trampoline accident, which made him very depressed. The next summer, Ray and I went to a drive-in movie with his sister and her date, and he thanked me profusely. Eventually, he married his nurse, so I was happy for him.

I ran into Gary Sauerteig in the Kodak cafeteria about 25 years later and we recognized each other instantly. We chatted for a few minutes, laughing about the boat ride. He's gone now, God rest his soul, but I'm glad I got to see him one more time.

Judy Gekoski's family often vacationed with us at the Becherer's. One year, Judy and I were walking along West Lake Road when a car with two young guys stopped. They asked us out that night and we eventually agreed after we asked them a lot of questions. They took us to East Lake Road where the asphalt ended and the dirt road began and wanted to shoot rabbits!! They had a shotgun in the car! We prayed that they wouldn't find any bunnies, and they didn't. Whew! However, the strangest thing happened. As we were outside the car on the dirt road, the four of us looked up toward the nighttime sky and about 100 feet above our heads was a huge, zigzagging light racing down on us, seemingly to chase us away! We were convinced it was an alien because of the way the ball of light *chased us*. We all jumped back in the car screaming, sped off, and the guys dropped us off back at our cottage. Yikes! We were all freaked out!

Another family that rented a Becherer's cottage with us at Honeoye Lake was the Church family from our neighborhood—Jerry, Audrey, Rodney, and Sue. One day, Sue and I walked West Lake Road into the town of Richmond (about 4 miles) and back. I was trying to whistle with my fingers but was never successful until we were close to returning to the cottages. The car that was going by stopped and started backing up. We screamed and started running down the hill to hide. Our bladders were so full at the time, we ended up peeing our pants. We couldn't stop laughing. During that week, we met some guys—Frank S., Jackie, and Ray. Jackie paddled a canoe to our dock and Mr. Church called him "Hiawatha." Frank drove up in a speed boat and he and I had a deep conversation about extraterrestrials at the dock, and he then asked me out. We went to a driving range in Canandaigua, NY, where I shocked him with the distance of my ball.

Mr. Church was blind, but he had a great sense of humor and a kind heart. My dad, the prankster, decided to play a trick on him. Jerry had a clothesline going from his cottage door to the outhouse (a flushing toilet in a stall), but Dad moved the clothesline so that Jerry ended up walking into a tree! Dad laughed his ass off, and Jerry called him, "That son of a bitch," but laughed along with him.

Back in my neighborhood, I had crushes on several boys, but everyone moved on to someone else. We would get together for parties in someone's house and play some kissing games, but it was never anything serious.

For one of my high school dances, I invited the guy across the street, Erwin K. Unfortunately, he came down with mono and had to back out. So, I called my cousin Bonnie, who agreed to loan me her boyfriend for the night, Paul F. Paul was a wonderful, considerate date and afterwards we went to a bowling alley and played candlepins for a couple of hours. We didn't want to piss off Bonnie by having "too much of a good time," so we said goodbye. Twenty years later, I had a phone conversation with Paul when he helped me with our mortgage, but I didn't put 2 and 2 together until I hung up the phone. Darn.

Austin P. was never a boyfriend or even a date, but he was part of our crowd from St. Jacob Street. He was a wrestler at Edison Tech and very well liked. A nice, sweet guy. One night, when I had my senior pictures with me, he grabbed them out of my hand. I freaked out, grabbed his wrist and twisted it, and he flew up into the air and then went flat on his back on the sidewalk. He was stunned. I was stunned. Did I just do that? I bet he was sorry to have his lights knocked out by a girl!

There was also a City Champion Wrestler from Benjamin Franklin High School who had his eyes on me—Phil N. He showed up at my house one Saturday afternoon while my parents were at Charlie's corner bar. I called Mom to let her know. Phil showed me how to do some evasive moves to get out of a wrestling hold. Uh huh. Before I knew it, I was in his hold. I broke free (with the newly learned evasive maneuver) and called Mom back.

"Ma, Phil is trying to attack me. You gotta come home." No one came home. (Mom's motto was "Fight your own battles.")

Again, Phil was getting out of control, and with his utter strength, I felt trapped. Again, I freed myself and called my mother to beg her to come home. No one came home. I finally convinced him to leave, and he did. Whew! Close call.

I met Dick C. when I was stood up by my date Frank D., who really cared more about fixing cars than me. I went to Durand Eastman Park with all my friends for a picnic and swimming, but I was alone. I went to the beach and met Dick and his friend Tom. At the time, I was going into my senior year of high school and Dick was attending Princeton University, a smart guy with a 4.0. We hit it off immediately. We wrote to each other during the school year and by the following June, at my graduation party, he pinned me. I was never so happy.

It didn't last. Although we dated throughout the summer by going to parks and having fun, I started to get "red flags." First, he was a terrible driver. I didn't drive at all, so I couldn't help. One evening, he ran over thousands of nails on the Lake Ontario State Parkway and flattened his tires. Couldn't be helped, I guess. He had one spare but then drove on the other rims! He drank a lot, too, and got behind the wheel. His sophisticated parents invited me over for dinner and I was a perfect guest, but Dick started talking about using marijuana to "open up his mind." It was the first time I heard him admit his usage. I never used anything illegal and never would. He and his father got into a heated argument and Dick stormed off to his room and locked the door, leaving me with his parents. Uh. Hello.

Then, in mid-August, Dick asked me if he could date a girl from Vassar—"F." What was I supposed to say? He was going to do it, and he did. The following week (just after I started my job at Kodak and my parents were on vacation at Honeoye Lake), he stopped by to break up with me. No hug. No kiss. Just goodbye. Wow. I cried my eyes out for a week.

In September, Dick sent me a letter, asking if I would like to come to Princeton for a weekend in October. I hoped it would be a reconciliation. It meant taking time off from my new job, but they allowed me two hours to catch a flight to Trenton, NJ, at the end of the day. I met a Kodak rep on the flight who offered to drive me to the train station to catch the train to Princeton.

I had never traveled alone, and it was confusing. Once in the train station, I asked for assistance, but no one would speak to me or even acknowledge me, not even the conductor. WTH. Luckily, I ended up on the right train, which rocked back and forth on the tracks like something from the 1920s. Maybe it was. Dick met me at the station and took me to the women's weekend dorm at one of the sorority houses. It was late, and I had to climb over sleeping bodies in the attic in the dark to find a place to stretch out. The girls from Vassar were rude, questioning what college I went to. I told them Eastman Kodak College, which stopped them in their tracks. The next day, my luggage was on the lawn. I was not allowed back in!

Dick offered his dorm (in other words, his bedroom). He did have the best dorm on campus: two-stories high, 2000 square feet, ultra-modern, six-bedroom building. But, I was a virgin and why would he think I was going to give it up for him when he just dumped me for another woman? Fuhgeddaboudit. It didn't happen. We did have fun at the Princeton-Brown football game and fraternity party on Saturday night, but we never dated again. When I was with my bridesmaids the night before my wedding, I ran into him at the Mardi Gras bar on Lake Ave, and he asked me to run away with him. HAHA! Right. He is still married to "F," by the way. Good for him.

A month after my Princeton trip, I met Jeff, and that changed my future.

Horseback Riding

WHEN I WAS 17 YEARS OLD, Judy Gekoski and I decided to go horseback riding at Heberle Stables. I wore black stretch pants to make it easier to mount whichever horse I was "given." I had never been on a horse before (except perhaps for a pony ride), but Judy had.

Heberle Stables was, and still is located adjacent to Ellison Park in Rochester, one of many Monroe County Parks in our area. Their horseback rides were 45 minutes long and were guided by the Heberle Stables staff. Their advertising says, "Our well-mannered trail horses make these treks suitable for the first-time rider to the most experienced."

The staff member, who was leading us that Saturday, instructed us on how to mount the horse. I was given a "gentle horse" since it was my first time. Even with stretch pants, it was much more difficult to throw my right leg over the horse's back than I expected. I felt a muscle pull, but it relaxed once I was on the horse.

We headed for the winding trail, which went through a park-like setting, although owned by Heberle. Some parts of the trail were quite narrow, with a hill on one side and gullies and drop-offs on the other. Roots poked through the dirt here and there, but I assumed that *"The horse knows the way,"* as the "Over the River and Through the Wood" song goes.

Me at Heberle Stables

I held onto the reins as the horses walked, and sometimes trotted along the trail. Suddenly there was a "drop." I assumed that the trail dipped, but I was firmly seated and holding onto the reins as my horse's head went down. He "recovered" and we kept going to the end of the ride and back to the stable.

Everyone suddenly circled around me as I dismounted. I couldn't figure out what they were doing!

One lady said, "Oh! You must be an expert horse rider!" I looked at her strangely and said, "No, not at all. It was my first time."

SEARCHING FOR SERENITY IN MY CRAZY LIFE

She was astonished. "Really? How did you stay on when your horse stumbled and fell to its knees?"

Stunned, I just said, "What?"

Apparently, my horse FELL. I had no idea! Everyone wanted to know if I was alright, and I was.

I never did go horseback riding again, but it wasn't due to what happened. I just never had the opportunity again.

Blizzard!

BACK ON JANUARY 29, 1966, Rochester was hit with a memorable blizzard that lasted about four days. Winds were more than 60 mph during the height of the storm, and at Fair Haven, NY, near Sodus they exceeded 100 mph. The snow drifted in roads, covered houses, and closed schools for a week. City side streets weren't cleared for days, but Mom still made us walk a half mile to Sunday Mass through the worst of the blizzard.

It was pretty exciting for us kids, though. After the storm subsided, I remember climbing the 6- or 7-foot-high snow piles by every driveway and going around our city block to find the highest one, which happened to be on Hudson Avenue where the plows had gone through.

At the end of the last day of the storm, there was an old guy who was walking toward our house from Charlie's corner bar with a six-pack of beer. He fell face first into the deep snow and couldn't get up. I didn't know if he was drunk or just unable to stand in the snow, with nothing to hold onto. I let Dad know. He went out to help and fell in the snow, too! So, I went out and helped them both up. The guy wanted to give Dad his beer, but Dad told him to keep it.

Since milk wasn't being delivered due to the storm (yes, we had Kunzer-Ellingwood Dairy deliver our milk to an insulated milkbox by the cellar door), Mom asked me to walk to a dairy on Joseph Avenue for milk. I grumbled a bit, but made the trek through snow-filled sidewalks. The snow stung my face, the cold air took my breath away, and my toes were frozen in my boots.

It was first time I had ever seen a snowmobile. The guy drove up and down Baumann Street saving stranded people in their cars, getting groceries for the old people, and just having fun zipping through the snow. It was quite a spectacle!!

Jeff and the Wedding

I MET JEFF IN THE 5th floor Kodak cafeteria, over a chow mein lunch. He was sitting with his co-workers Ron and Pete from Camera Works. I was eating with my girlfriend Dolores N., who was from my neighborhood and went to high school with me. She was a secretary in Radiology Markets and I was also a secretary, but in Motion Picture & Audiovisual Markets (MP&AV).

Dolores was sweet and kind, but very nervous, and she had good reason to be. On the day of our Senior Picnic, her mom committed suicide and Dolores and her brother found her. I stayed the night with her and the following day. Mom called the school and explained the situation. Then during our Senior Prom, her boyfriend broke up with her. Two traumatic events in three weeks. A month later, we both ended up getting jobs at Kodak's corporate offices and started going to lunch together every day.

When I interviewed at Kodak (set up by my high school counselor), the Personnel contact was an elderly woman who thought that I was lying when I said I was good at organization, shorthand, and typing. (She thought I was full of B.S.!) She refused to hire me. However, there was another interviewer in the cubicle next to hers (Betty Brownell) who heard every word. She called me into her office and hired me on the spot. I did have to take a typing test on a 1930s machine on which the keys kept falling off, but I passed. I had to go through Secretarial Services before getting a permanent job. My first supervisor changed my name to Elly, and that's the name I kept for the rest of my life. My first assignment was to organize Kodak patents, which I did. A couple of months later, I accepted the job in MP&AV.

It was close to Thanksgiving in 1966 when I noticed the guys in the cafeteria looking over at Dolores and me. I found out later that they were trying to look up our miniskirts. Nice. Jeff came over and introduced himself. He was extremely thin, with slicked-back hair, but had a nice, big smile. He asked me if I would like to go out to a movie on Thanksgiving night to see *The Greatest Story Ever Told*. I knew my relatives would be at my house to see Marcia, who was home from the convent for the day, but I didn't think they'd miss me. So I agreed.

After that date, Jeff had my number and would call every night. Many times Mom and I were in the middle of cleaning up the kitchen, so I'd cut the conversation short, sometimes on purpose. I wasn't thrilled that he was a smoker. It just wasn't my thing. However, he did invite me to go out for dinner to a very expensive, very fancy restaurant (Page One on East Main Street). I agreed and bought a turquoise chiffon dress just for the occasion. The meal was exquisite; and a trio played "The Shadow of Your Smile" just for me. It was very romantic. We became an "item."

We dated exclusively over the next five months. It turned out that he didn't have much money, but he had excellent skills, a steady Kodak job, and goals to become an architectural or mechanical engineer. His father had thrown him out of the house because he chose to get a job instead of stay home and take care of his mom, who had debilitating MS. So, he was living in a boarding house near Taylor Instruments. On our first date, he had an old Corvair, but he saved up enough money for a down payment on a new, yellow-with-black-stripe Chevy Camero, which he was very proud of.

In April, we packed a peanut butter and jelly sandwich lunch, and went to the Maplewood Rose Gardens. There he proposed, giving me a beautiful diamond engagement ring (I picked it out, actually). I said yes. That weekend, we went to his house, snuck in, and showed his mom my ring. She couldn't speak, but her face brightened and she smiled. Then we got caught by his dad and we were thrown out.

In September 1967, Jeff enlisted in the United States Air Force, hoping to hone his drafting skills and better his career opportunities. I didn't see him again for half a year or more.

Meanwhile, I planned the entire wedding. I wanted a typical Polish wedding with Polish food and a Polish band— Ray Serafin and his Orchestra. I picked out the first gown I saw, a full "princess" gown with lace and long sleeves. I asked my forever-girlfriend Judy Gekoski to be my maid of honor but she was living at Plattsburgh AFB in New York with her husband Erwin, and couldn't afford it, so I asked my cousin Bonnie. She said yes. Then Judy came back and said her aunt would pay for it, but by then I had a maid of honor. She was very, very upset. I was upset as well because I had hurt her feelings. Dolores was a bridesmaid, and Jeff's best friend Paul (Skip) Grieco was his best man.

Jeff's immediate family did not attend the wedding, but his two aunts and uncles came. It meant a lot.

Mickey was our altar boy. He kept making faces during the ceremony, which cracked me up. Msgr. Quinn told us we couldn't kiss, but we did anyway, much to his chagrin. The one thing I'm totally embarrassed about—I didn't know we were supposed to offer the church money. My mother was shocked at my lack of etiquette. I didn't know! I had never gotten married before! Why didn't she tell me? I made up for it.

Our Wedding

We had pictures taken in Durand Eastman Park, a cocktail party back at the house, followed by the reception at the Ukrainian Civic Center on Joseph Avenue. My pen pal (since age 12), Carmen, attended, coming from South Bend, Indiana. We are still writing today!

The only thing that "went wrong" was that our new VW Squareback was filled with newspapers when we left the reception and my gown and all my clothes on my honeymoon were ruined by the newsprint. I was not a happy camper.

We had a lovely honeymoon on Cape Cod. The life-long story that Jeff won't drop was that I couldn't eat the spicy Portuguese fish so I traded him for his swordfish. He claims that he can never order swordfish because I always steal it from him. ONCE, I tell you. It happened ONCE.

Back in Rochester, we said tearful goodbyes to the family (especially Patty), and started off for our new life in Sumter, SC, where Jeff was stationed at Shaw Air Force Base.

Life on
N. Salem Avenue

Sumter, SC
1968-1971

Starting a New Life

JEFF HAD ALREADY FOUND an apartment 12 miles away from Shaw Air Force Base in the city of Sumter, SC, before I moved down there. Rent was $65/month. I also sent him money to buy a car, so he could drive to and from the Base.

North Salem Avenue, Sumter, SC

When I arrived in Sumter, I carried Jeff over the threshold because he was only 117 pounds and I had 10 pounds on him.

The apartment was upstairs in the back of an old brick home on North Salem Avenue, owned by widow Mrs. Lillian Brailsford. There was an outside wooden staircase that took us to our door, and a clothesline on a pulley that stretched to the garage. The living room had a couch with a spring sticking out of it, a chair, and a built-in knickknack shelf. The kitchen had linoleum that was rippled, an electric stove, sink, table and chairs, and a narrow pantry cabinet. The bathroom had a tub (no shower). But the bedroom stretched out the entire front of the house. There was a dresser, a makeup vanity and mirror, a rocking chair, a double bed, and lots of extra room for a crib, a TV, or anything else. And it had an *air conditioner*. We also had a walk-in closet that led to the attic, which we used for storage.

I woke up the first morning hearing the bluejays squawking in the pecan tree. It was heavenly. And hot. We turned on the "Pig Report" (because we only had one TV station) and listened to the commercial for fertilizer: *"Wake up! Wake up! It's time to fertilize!"* It made us laugh.

We had to get up early because Jeff had to be at the Base on time. I decided to make him a breakfast like Dad always had—bacon, eggs, toast, and coffee. I plugged in our new Farberware percolator. When Jeff came out into the kitchen, he asked what was burning. It was the coffee pot! He opened it and exclaimed, "You forgot to add the water!" I looked at him like he was an alien, replying, "Oh, I didn't know I had to. Where does it come from?" He knew he was in trouble. He had a glass of Tang and went to work.

We arrived in Sumter at the time when Civil Rights were paramount. Martin Luther King had just been assassinated. We originally saw signs that read, "This water spigot is for white men only." And "This park is dedicated to the white men of the Confederacy." And small restaurants that had placards in the window printed with "Whites Only." If a black man saw a white woman walking on the same sidewalk, he would cross the road. It was like that everywhere, but "things they were a-changin'." Not long afterwards, all those signs were required to be removed, and they were.

I made friends with another girl—Sharon C.—who got married to an Air Force man the same day we did in a church of the same name and rented a house on the same street as ours. Freaky. She invited me over for daily morning coffee, which relieved a lot of loneliness. I think I overstayed my welcome after visiting every day, though, as she wasn't as welcoming.

In August we received a telegram that Jeff's mother had passed away a few weeks earlier. He was devastated, but there was nothing he could do.

I had to find a job, so I checked the employment opportunities in the newspaper. There was secretarial job at the Episcopal Church, and another at Sumter Fuel and Ice. I called and set up times for interviews. The minister at the Episcopal Church on Main Street wasn't thrilled that I was a Yankee, an Air Force wife, and a Catholic. I didn't get the job. The next day, I walked to Sumter Fuel and Ice, a long way to walk in a strange town. They were very blunt, saying they didn't want a Yankee. When I left there, I stood on the sidewalk and just cried. A homeless man came up to me and had pity on me. He asked me what was wrong and listened to every word. He assured me that I would find something soon. God bless him. I'll always remember his kindness.

Another day I interviewed for Morehouse-McKenzie Company, a wholesale plumbing and supply company, and got the job. They couldn't afford to pay my Kodak salary of a whopping $109/week, but they could pay me $40/week. I took it.

I took dictation, typed letters, kept inventory records, ordered product, and answered the phones. My fellow employees were all Baptist except for Mr. Morehouse, who was Episcopalian. Salesmen Otto and Bob used to tease me saying, "Light a candle for me, Mz. Elly," and "I'll dance at your next wedding," because, of course, they didn't dance. Cecil, the head salesperson, was all business. He flipped one day when I ordered a large quantity of black pipe, per dictation, when the boss was in Hawaii on business. Cecil ended up calling long distance to check with the boss. I was correct. Cecil's worry stemmed from an earlier secretary who ordered 45 red tubs for the Holiday Inn. She meant to order 5 and the company was stuck with 40 red tubs. Mildred, the bookkeeper, had polio and used crutches, but she never complained. Our truck driver Ramsey was black, and he would come into the office for his paycheck every Friday, with his hat off and his eyes down. We tried to get him to smile and loosen up, but he wouldn't change. Too much history there. There was a young black boy who would come in and sell "goobers" in a bag every week. I always bought some, even though I didn't like the wet consistency of his peanuts. And John, the warehouse and counter man, had me laughing one day. We both answered the phone at the same time. I tried to tell him that I'd handle the call, but he thought

I was the caller and insisted that "he" was the Morehouse-McKenzie man. I never did get through to him. oy.

A few months down the road, I discovered that I was pregnant and told my Mom, who told everyone else. Unfortunately, a few days later as I was walking to take the company deposit to the bank, I felt cramping and lost the baby that night. It wasn't long, though, before I was pregnant again. This time Mom didn't tell anyone and the baby was a surprise to the family back home. I missed out on a baby shower, but I had lots of S&H Green Stamps to buy all the necessities.

I was sick with a bad cold when my due date came around. I was no longer working. Jeff tried to make me laugh to induce labor and took me for a ride on a bumpy road. That night, I stayed awake because I couldn't breathe, and by 5 a.m., I knew it was time to go. On November 6, 1969, the temperature was only 18°, frigid for South Carolina. I shivered all the way to the hospital, and my labor stopped. When we got there, I remembered that I hadn't fed our cat Rusty, so I sent Jeff back home while I checked myself in. I thought he would come right back, but he stopped in to see Sharon and have a cup of coffee. He thought he had time.

At 6 a.m. I was almost fully dilated. At 8 a.m. I started hard labor. At 9:45 a.m. Eric Andrew Stevens was born. Jeff made it back just in time. They handed Eric to him first, and I was insanely jealous. It took a while to get over that.

Eric caught my cold, unfortunately, and I spent an entire month rocking him all night so that he could breathe. My family came down for the baptism and stayed a few days. I didn't get any extra rest with all those people in our tiny apartment.

Jeff, Me and Eric (on Baumann Street)

I think they were shocked at how run-down our apartment was, too. It didn't matter to me unless a flying tree cockroach got inside. One night, a cockroach was crawling on the ceiling and fell on my face while I was in bed. I screamed! We'd spray them with Raid and they'd disintegrate in the toilet.

Once, a black-widow spider was on our front door, so we went in and out through Mrs. Brailsford's apartment until, finally, we spray-painted the spider and he fell to the ground. We also had rattlesnakes in the yard. Speaking of snakes, there was an older man, Mr. Hood, who rented a room downstairs and he had a pet boa constrictor.

He caught wild birds for it to eat, which upset me. Why not rodents? I got to hold the snake once.

At Christmas, there was an ice storm that left us without power for three days. Mrs. Brailsford cooked for everyone in her fireplace, making catfish stew and other southern delicacies. She declared Eric to be an engineer. She must have been psychic!

After the holidays, I went back to Morehouse-McKenzie to train a new secretary. I knew they were in trouble. One day she had a black eye; another day she was hung over. I did my best. On the first day, Jeff and I took Eric to the Base Nursery with a diaper bag full of formula, diapers, and other necessities. When I picked him up at 5:30 p.m., he was screaming bloody murder. **They never fed him; never changed him!** And he had such a bad diaper burn that it had to be treated by a professional. I was so angry! I yelled at them but no one said a word. I should have reported them to Base officials. (Why didn't I?) Luckily, Sharon C. was a nurse and she gave me burn medication to use for a week. Eric never went back to the Base Nursery.

Eric was a colicky baby and sometimes a drive in the car would help him fall asleep. One warm night, Eric was crying a lot so we got into our VW Squareback and just drove around aimlessly. We turned down an old dirt road and saw hundreds of cars. Cars were pulling in back of us as well, so we couldn't just turn around. Then we saw them. Hundreds of men in white sheets with pointy heads gathered in the field—The Ku Klux Klan! Holy crap! They were having a bonfire and rally! I was terrified! We just kept driving, hoping the road would take us back to a familiar highway, and it did.

The Detective

THERE WAS A KNOCK at the door one hot evening, when it was still light outside. Jeff and I looked at each other, as it was quite odd to have company, especially unexpected company. We were watching TV and the baby was sleeping. I answered the door to find an unfamiliar man standing there. I looked in the driveway and saw a red Ford Mustang parked there, with clothes hanging from a rod in the back seat. It looked like there was a woman sitting in the passenger seat, but I couldn't see her clearly.

He said he was sent by our mutual friends down the road (we did know one couple). He was selling Grolier Encyclopedias. I looked at Jeff and he looked at me and we agreed to hear his spiel. He said he was very thirsty, so I got him a glass of water. He put the glass down on our speaker. It left a water ring, which made us upset. Then he had to use the bathroom. Okay... Then we listened while he talked about having all this information for our baby as he grew up and went to school. "You need encyclopedias," he informed us.

He also warned us that he was not "playing a game." We would be signing a contract and would give him a down payment and pay a certain amount each month.

Jeff thought I wanted the encyclopedias; I thought he wanted them. We signed the contract, and the salesman left with our check.

I said to Jeff, "Well, you got your encyclopedias."

He responded, "Mine? I thought you wanted them!"

"No, I didn't want them!"

We got out the Grolier contract and read it carefully. We had three full days to cancel.

The next day I went into work at Morehouse-McKenzie, and called Grolier as soon as I was able. The telephone rep asked me the name of the salesman, which I read off to her from the contract. She put me on hold.

A few minutes later, she came back on the phone and said, "That particular salesman is not licensed to sell in the state of South Carolina. I'm afraid he may have taken your check for his own use. If I were you, I'd put a stop on it immediately. I will notify the police in Sumter."

I replied, "Before you call the police, I know what car he was driving. Let us check out the three motels in town."

I called my bank but the check had already been cashed. Then, that night, Jeff and I drove over to the Holiday Inn (the only hotel in town with red bathtubs, by the way). We didn't have to look any further. There was the Mustang, still with clothes on a rod in the back seat. I went back home, called Grolier, and gave them the information along with his license plate number.

The next day Grolier called me back to say that the salesman lost his job and had been arrested and jailed. Grolier put a check in the mail to me and cancelled the contract with their apologies.

Three nights later, as we were having dinner, the wall phone rang and I answered. It was the salesman.

"What are you, a fucking detective? I just got out of jail, you BITCH!"

I hung up. Chalk one up for the good guys.

The Cake

MRS. BRAILSFORD WAS A good cook. In fact, she worked for the Sumter School District in the elementary school cafeteria. I had some issues when watching her flour catfish and saw that there were wiggling weevils in the flour. As a result, I refrained from trying any.

But she had a wonderful cake recipe, from scratch, that she wanted to share with me. It was all typed up on a sheet of typing paper. I decided to try it.

First of all, I was not an experienced cook or baker, to say the least. Actually, I knew nothing. I went to the Winn Dixie at the corner of our street and bought the ingredients. You'd think that would be enough for a good result, but you'd be wrong. I bought self-rising flour instead of cake flour or even regular flour, along with baking powder.

I preheated my oven. I mixed the ingredients. There seemed to be an awful lot of batter. I put it in a rectangular cake pan and realized it was too full. I got out a second cake pan and filled that to the brim, too. I put them in the oven. I set the timer, but I decided to check on the cake a few times.

When I opened the oven, I was shocked. There was the cake, like a balloon in my oven! I had to start pulling it out in sections! It was just like the *I Love Lucy* episode when she pulled a cake out of her oven and kept pulling and pulling it out, and it just wasn't stopping! When I got the cake down to a reasonable size, it seemed to finish baking.

That night when we tried a piece, it was like a rock. Truly, a rock. I tried to cut it with a knife and fork, but I couldn't even get a fork into it. I looked at the recipe one more time and realized I used the wrong flour, but also that it was a recipe for the ***entire elementary school!!***

I didn't want Mrs. Brailsford to know my cake was such a failure so, after darkness, Jeff and I silently crept down the long staircase to the backyard (shaking a stick to scare away the rattlesnakes), went behind the garage, dug a hole, and buried the cake. I hoped she'd never notice the mound of dirt.

Decades later, I went onto Google Earth and found where the house on North Salem Avenue used to be. The entire row of old houses was gone, and replaced by some sort of strip building—perhaps for apartments, or offices, or stores. I wondered if a bulldozer operator might have unearthed my cake during construction and thought, perhaps, it was a prehistoric fossil. Just maybe.

Life on
Brambury Drive

Rochester, NY
1971-1974

Back in Rochester

IN JULY 1971, I returned to Rochester with Eric to find an apartment, while Jeff continued his stint in South Carolina for two more months. We had our brand-new, South Carolina-built, solid oak bedroom furniture shipped by tractor trailer to Aunt Helen's Kunzer-Ellingwood Dairy warehouse behind her house on Durnan Street until I found a place to live. The truck driver was not happy that he had to back into her narrow driveway to the dairy warehouse, but he did it.

Besides Helen's son Duane, my cousin Scotty was also living with her, as well as her mom, my Grandma Fedyk. Grandpa Fedyk had died back in 1956, and Aunt Helen's husband Eugene had died shortly thereafter. Scotty, who was my age, had just gotten out of the Merchant Marines and had a drug problem. He was in a methadone treatment program in Rochester. Aunt Helen took him in.

On July 16, my brother Mickey went to visit Aunt Helen and saw Scotty sleeping on a glider in the enclosed back porch. He didn't think anything of it. It turned out that he had passed away.

When Scotty was born, his mother died in a car accident and my Uncle Mitch remarried. As Dad told us, he almost adopted Scotty, because he was concerned about his care. Scotty grew up to be a nervous, insecure child and man. When Dad went to Scotty's funeral, he got quite drunk (I didn't go because I had to take care of Eric) and he blamed himself for his death. I had never seen my Dad like that. Ever.

I soon found a two-bedroom apartment on Brambury Drive on the edge of Irondequoit and Rochester, and took out a three-year lease. There was a gigantic courtyard so Eric could ride his Fisher Price Creative Coaster on the sidewalk and never get near a street. It was perfect for kids! I made friends with my upstairs neighbor, Marcie W, and another mother of two, Carole D. I got the first tan in my life by watching Eric play outside all summer.

Eric was a little boy in every sense. He loved racing cars, loved to build things and to tear things apart to see how they worked. One morning I went to take a shower, and when I got out, I found him taking off all the doors to the kitchen cabinets with a screwdriver. He was 18 months old. On a day when we were going to have our picture taken for his Daddy, I found him on top of the bathroom sink, trying to "shave" his face with shaving cream. And when he rode his Creative Coaster around the courtyard, he'd make such sharp turns, it would overturn his "car." Carole pulled me aside and advised me that she had noticed a balance issue with him. I laughed, knowing he did it on purpose!

Carole's son Chris was about 2 years old when he cried out that there was a "lobster" at the bird feeder. We all looked. It was a rat! We had issues with rats coming from the Two Guys department store's dumpsters so Carole called her neighbor, Mr. McDermott, who shot the rat.

Before I was married, I used to write to servicemen during the Viet Nam War. One serviceman was someone I knew from Kodak and he showed my picture to his Navy buddy, Jerry M. I ended up writing to him as well. Jerry and I remained friends even after we both married, and he visited me on several occasions, once when we lived on Brambury Drive. One day we decided to take my bike to Seneca Park and take turns riding it on the circular road. The only problem was that I had no experience riding down steep hills. I almost lost control of my bike and thought I was going to crash and die. However, I managed to not kill myself. The next day we took Eric to the carousel at Charlotte Beach. I attempted to get on a moving carousel horse, hit my thigh on the footrest, and created an enormous bruise that lasted months. You can't take me anywhere!

The serviceman I knew from Kodak ended up giving me obscene phone calls when I moved into the apartment, until I recognized his voice on the second call. He couldn't believe that I knew who it was after not seeing him for 3-4 years. Don't pull that on me!

A few weeks after Jerry's visit, I removed everything from the top of my dresser to dust it. I knocked over the bottle of the Chanel No. 5 perfume that he had given me as a thank you and it spilled everywhere. It smelled like a French whore house.

Another time I left Eric alone in the bedroom for a few minutes after I cleaned off the dresser (once again). When I came back in, I pushed the door open and a long-stem-rose vase that I had placed behind the door fell over and broke into a million pieces. Eric held his breath and looked at me in total fear, thinking he was going to get a spanking.

"Oh no!! I broke my vase!" I said. "It was Mommy's fault. I shouldn't have left it there." I never saw him look so relieved.

When Eric turned 3, it was time for me to go back to work. Carole agreed to babysit for him. I interviewed at the McDonald's just up the road. I was alone in the back office with the 20-something-year-old manager, who undressed me with his eyes and asked me what my bra size was. I decided I didn't want to work there. I went back to Kodak and got a secretarial job in Market Research & Analysis, working for a 40-year-old man named Willard W. and his "specialist," Pat M. We all became friends for life.

About six months later, Jeanne Buell joined the group. We recognized each other from Nazareth Academy, although we had never spoken to each other. From Day One, we became best friends. I stopped going to lunch with Dolores and started going to lunch with Jeanne. We had lunch every day for 30 years, and, er, sometimes a cocktail. (Once we split a bottle of wine with another of Willard's specialists, Frank K. at the Crossroads Park in downtown Rochester. Fun times.)

After the lease was up on our apartment, we extended it month by month until we found somewhere else to move. We went to a Realtor who, that night, showed us a ranch house in Greece on Fairview Court. We put in an offer and it was accepted.

Life on
Fairview Court

Greece, NY
1974-1981

Turning 30

I DOUBT THAT ANYONE HAS EVER had a more stressful 30th birthday. Looking back over four decades ago, it seems like yesterday.

Unfortunately, that day I woke up with my "monthly friend" and felt some stomach cramping and mild bloating. I thought, *"It had to show up on my birthday. Swell."* I hoped the rest of the day would be better.

It was a surprisingly lovely April day, a real gift. Even though I lived near Lake Ontario, where northwest winds often made bundling up a necessity in spring, I didn't need a jacket. I wore a pink miniskirt, a white blouse with ruffled sleeves and collar, and pink high heels. Jeff kindly dropped me off at the bus stop so I didn't have to hike a half-mile in my fragile shoes.

At work, my co-worker and Avon lady, Mary-Helen Maginn, delivered the new ring I had ordered—a faux topaz with a rhinestone on either side and set in silverplate—and I put it on with excitement. My day was getting better!

Two of my bosses, Frank and Jeanne, treated me to a birthday lunch at an Italian restaurant where we all had veal parmesan sandwiches and a glass of wine. In addition,

Jeanne gave me a birthday gift—a novel that I had been anxious to read.

Shortly after we returned to the office, my birthday started going downhill. (Is that why they call 30 *"over the hill"?*)

While I was in Jeanne's office thanking her for lunch and the book, she confessed that her stomach was feeling queasy. She grabbed her trash basket, lowered her head, and promptly threw up! I backed up, thinking she had the flu and I didn't want to catch it. She decided to go home. I wondered how she could drive the distance without getting sick again.

Frank came out of his office and headed down the aisle. He was complaining that he didn't feel so hot either. When he heard about Jeanne, he decided to leave before getting sick. (Thank goodness.) I had no desire to witness that again. It was very peculiar that they both got sick within an hour of eating lunch. I wondered if I were next.

Not long after Frank left, the same feeling came over me and I decided it would be best if I went home. I called Jeff to let him know. I grabbed my purse and new novel and headed to the bus stop. There wasn't any shelter or bench at the stop, so I stood and waited a half hour for my bus to arrive. I kept taking deep breaths, hoping I wouldn't get sick. Once the bus picked me up, it was another half hour before I arrived at the stop nearest to my house. Luckily, I made the trip without getting sick in my seat. I held my book tightly to my stomach.

I walked up Beach Avenue and crossed at Alpha Street. My high heels were killing my toes. Oh, the price of vanity!

Out of the corner of my eye, I saw a nice-looking guy walking on the other side of the street, heading toward Beach Avenue. Yes, as sick as I was, I still looked. As he got closer, I noticed that he was slim, in his mid-20s I guessed, had light brown hair, and a pleasant face. I obviously was not looking where I was walking, however. Suddenly, I felt my ankle twist in pain and I was starting to collapse. I tried unsuccessfully to regain my balance, but gravity would not allow me to stop the fall once it started. My book flew in the air and I stretched out my hand to stop my fall. Big mistake. I landed awkwardly on a twisted right hand, shooting intense pain signals to my brain. I was sure I had broken my hand or at least a few fingers. I sat up, holding my right hand and trying to suppress the pain. I saw that my pantyhose was ruined, exposing a number of runs, my skirt was dirty where I fell, and my palm was scraped up. The contents of my purse were scattered on the ground alongside my book, which seemed to be undamaged.

I noticed a hunk of rock laying next to me on the broken and heaved sidewalk. I must have stepped on it. I tried to stand up and quickly found that I was in too much pain.

To my utter astonishment, the young man from across the street ran to my side. "Mrs. Stevens! Mrs. Stevens!" he cried. "Are you alright?"

I thought, *"He knows my name? Who is he? And he's calling me Mrs.? Man, I feel OLD."*

"I think something is broken," I responded, gasping for breath.

"Let me help you. If you can make it to the store here, we'll get you a chair to sit down on." There was a tiny mom-and-pop grocery store next to where I had fallen. I had never gone in there before and didn't know what to expect. However, I didn't have any better ideas and I let him take command of the situation. He helped me to my feet and handed me the purse and book that I had tossed in my fall.

I felt quite disoriented, but managed to hobble into the store. He asked the store owner, a woman in her sixties, to get me a chair and some water. She complied. She had a terrified look on her face. I thought, *"I must really be in bad shape!"*

Handing me the water cup, she reluctantly asked, "Did you fall in front of my store?"

"So that's why she's afraid!" I thought.

"No, next door." I gasped in between swallows. "Stepped on a rock." There was a notable sigh of relief and she relaxed now that she knew I wouldn't be suing her. I held up my hand to view it; it was purple and swelling fast.

"Oh no!" I cried. "My new ring! Take it off!" I pleaded. It was like a tourniquet on my swelling finger.

The young man said, "No, I can't. Your finger may be broken!"

"Oh, please," I begged. "I don't care about my finger! I don't want them to cut off the ring. I just got it today!"

Thinking that I would have to get a broken bone reset anyway, he finally gave in and wiggled the ring free.

"If you give me your husband's phone number, I'll call him. He can meet us at the hospital."

"Hospital?"

"Yes, you really need to have someone look at your hand. I'll get my car and drive you there."

My mind went blank trying to think of Jeff's name and number. Oh, God. It took a couple minutes of searching my brain, but I finally came up with the information. He made a phone call from the store, then ran off to get his car. I still didn't know who he was, where he lived, or how he knew my name.

I don't remember much of the car ride to the hospital, but my white knight told me where he lived. Would you believe, cater-corner from our house? I had never seen him before, but he had obviously seen me! He also mentioned that he was getting married in two weeks. The facts seemed to blur in my mind. I could only think of the pain in my hand.

We arrived at Rochester General Hospital's emergency room around 3:30 p.m. and walked up to the receptionist.

"Name?" she asked without concern.

I furnished my full name.

"Address?"

I gave it to her.

"Phone number?"

Supplied.

"Age?"

"What did she ask me? Age? Not date of birth? What am I going to say???"

I mumbled, "Thirty."

"I'm sorry. I didn't hear you. Could you repeat that?"

I turned my head away from the young man, put my good hand up to my mouth, and whispered, "Thirty."

"Thirty? Did you say 'thirty'?" she questioned loudly.

He looked at me incredulously, "Thirty?"

I shrunk into the floor tile, feeling really old and decrepit. "Yes, thirty," I said to the nurse without looking at my rescuer.

"I didn't think you were *that* old!" he exclaimed.

87

Oh God.

The hospital nurses took one look at me and I heard them say amongst themselves, "She doesn't look good. We'd better get her in right away." They whisked me off. I didn't know what hurt the worst: my swollen, purple hand, my twisted ankle, my queasy stomach, my period cramps, or my pride. I was sure it was my pride.

They x-rayed my hand and determined that nothing was broken. It was "just" a bad sprain that would heal in about six months.

"Six months! No gardening. No bicycling. No use of my hand for the entire summer!" I moaned to myself.

They gave me a tetanus shot in my good arm. *"Oh, good. Now another part of my body hurts."*

"We'll notify Dr. Gangemi and let him know that we've treated you," the nurse assured.

Jeff arrived and we thanked the young man before he scooted out the door and out of my life.

Me at 30

When I was feeling better a few days later, I bought a bottle of champagne and took it over to his house. His mother cautiously opened the door about four inches. I explained that he had helped me and I wanted to thank him.

"He's getting married next week," she informed me as if I were the devil incarnate and telling me of their nuptials would protect them from my evil eye.

"Yes, I know. He and his wife can enjoy this champagne. Please tell him I said thank you."

I never saw him again. I'm not sure I ever wanted to. Thirty. How mortifying!

Eric's Adventures

AS PART OF OUR routine in the morning before Eric's preschool, Jeff would drive the two of us up to the corner of Stutson Street and Lake Ave and let us off. Then Eric and I would cross the street to the church where he had day care. Then I would walk back across the street to the bus stop and catch the Lake Avenue bus to work.

One morning, Eric was lollygagging as we got out of Jeff's car. I said, "Hurry up. I have to catch the bus!" He stopped for a moment, looked at me, and asked, "How do you catch a bus?" I laughed to myself, trying to put myself in his shoes, imagining a person running and grabbing the bus bumper! Haha! I explained that I didn't really catch it; I just had to be at the bus stop when it came down the street.

When he attended kindergarten, he was enrolled in another church program on St. Paul Street in inner city. Jeff would drive us there in the morning and I would walk in with him. After the first morning, Eric became very agitated and clingy and I had to tear his hand off my clothes, my purse, my hand, etc. I had no idea why he was acting so afraid. I knew he made friends with a very tall, very strong, black kid named Douglas, so the clinginess was very surprising.

On the fifth day when I went to pick him up after work, he had a large cut on his cheek! I was told that another boy, who was very jealous of Eric, attacked him every morning after I dropped him off. Why I had not been told before that day, I never understood. The kindergarten teacher told me that they expelled the other boy and there would not be any further attacks. The cut created a scar that lasted forever.

Eric's Snowman

When Eric was in the first grade, he started all-day sessions at No. 38 School on Latta Road. He had an after-school babysitter—Mamie Thomas—who watched multiple children at her house around the corner from us. She was always on top of things. One day, when the weather was still pleasant, she waited for Eric's bus to arrive. When it became late, she was a bit concerned, but figured it would show up. After 45 minutes, she knew something was wrong.

Mamie called me at work and said, "Ella, Eric's bus hasn't shown up yet! I'm very concerned."

I was in a quandary because I took the city bus to work and had no way to get home quickly. Plus, buses didn't run frequently during the day. I asked if she could call the school, which she did. About 45 minutes later she called back to say that the bus had shown up. Apparently, the bus driver totally forgot to make Eric's stop. Eric didn't seem to care that he was riding all over town and just took it in stride. If he was stressed, he never mentioned it. I think he just thought it was curious that the bus hadn't gotten to his street yet.

The bus driver was very apologetic, but the situation could have been worse. He could have taken the bus back to the bus lot and left Eric there. We were just grateful he was back at Mamie's safe and sound.

In later years at School 38, Eric also had to go to Religious Education at Holy Cross School on Lake Avenue. Because I had to get him to this class, I had to learn to drive. (Yes, I was 29 years old.) It was exciting for me, because I finally had independence—and a new 1976 8-cylinder, dual-exhaust, special edition, silver Chevy Nova Medalist sedan! Up until then, Jeff wanted to drive me everywhere. Oh well! Now I had my own wheels!

I would question Eric when he got home from religious ed. "What did you learn today? What did you do? Who came to talk to you?" He would usually shrug his shoulders and just answer "I don't know." One night after class he told me that they played a game where the first person was told a story and he repeated it to the next student, and so on. The last kid stood up and repeated what he heard and it was totally messed up and everyone laughed. I asked what the subject was. He said, "Astronauts going to the moon." I was shocked that it was not a Bible story and truly wondered what he was getting out of this class.

When he grew old enough to make his first Holy Communion, I discovered that they did things quite differently than they did when I was growing up. No 7-year-old boys wearing white shirts and ties, no classes marching into church and singing hymns, and no lines going up to the Communion rail (long gone!), no hands folded in reverence to receive the Holy Wafer. Instead, the parent had to make an appointment with the parish priest who would ask the candidate (Eric) questions to determine if he was ready for the sacrament. If he was ready, the student would go up for communion alone or with his parents.

I took Eric to meet the priest, an impatient old man with a round, ruddy face. Eric was TERRIFIED! He rarely ever spoke to adults and this was even scarier because he had to know the answers to the questions. Eric refused to open his mouth, but stared at his hands in absolute terror. He never answered a single question and the priest was getting more and more angry. I told him that he was shy, but he didn't want to hear it. His last question was, "Is Jesus God or man?" I kicked Eric's shoe and he blurted out, "Man!" Oh shit. The wrong answer. The priest was purple with rage and screamed that Eric was not ready for communion. I was in shock and the priest screamed, "Fine! Let him make his communion! I don't care!!" and bolted out of the room, leaving us frozen to our chairs. When I realized he was not coming back, we left, and Eric made his communion the following Sunday.

It might have been the last time Eric took communion. After that, he begged not to go to church and ended up staying home with his dad. I felt like such a failure, all because of that nasty priest! All the priests in my youth were kind and gentle to children. It really gave Eric a terrible view of religion. It made me very sad.

Eric also joined the Cub Scouts. He went to his den meetings a few streets from our house. One night I went to pick him up and his glasses were broken. He and another kid were fooling around and fighting when the glasses snapped. I was not happy.

He made several projects in the scouts to earn his badges. He made a turkey out of pipe cleaners and feathers, a solar system exhibit, and a paper mâché volcano, all of which were taken to the Scout Show at the Dome Arena. They all disappeared, never to be seen again, even though Eric and I stayed at the booth for the whole day. I was upset but, most importantly, he was devastated. His den leader had no excuse either.

Toward the end of the school year, the den leader requested that both parents attend the next meeting to discuss an upcoming event. Jeff could not go to the meeting because he attended night classes at Rochester Institute of Technology, but I went. It wasn't good enough. The parents were told, that if BOTH parents did not attend, the scout would not be permitted to attend the event at Seabreeze Amusement Park. They were firm. Eric was punished for not having both parents there and was not allowed to attend. I was furious and had a few choice words for them. Jerks!

On the night they were supposed to receive their badges, Eric was upset. The den leader explained to them that there was a "needy" den and, due to a shortage of badges, all their earned badges would go to the needy den instead. Eric never received a single badge. I was so furious, I wrote to the head council, but never heard another thing. I refused to send Eric back to scouts the following year.

When Eric was a young teen, we made arrangements to put him on a plane to visit his cousin Josh in Virginia. He would be guided by an airport employee when he had to switch planes and met at the final airport by Josh's mom, Jeff's sister, Lynda.

What I didn't realize was that the second plane was a prop job. Apparently, it rattled and shook and dropped in the air currents, making Eric terrified. He never wanted to fly again as long as he lived (although he did in his 30s, when he and his family flew to Disney World).

Eric and I both had bicycles, and one Sunday morning in the summer, we rode them to Charlotte Beach, about a half mile away. As we were winding through the park's sidewalks, I noticed movement on top of one of the picnic tables. It was a man and a woman engaged in sex! OMG. I got him out of there, fast.

On one other ride, just as we were headed home, a dog came out from a driveway, barking and growling. He ran after me on my bike, and clamped onto my right calf with his jaw. I tried to shake him off, but couldn't. Finally, after dragging him several houses, he let go and I rode home. I cleaned up the bites and bandaged them, but I never got on my bike again.

Kodak Moments

Cigars

MY BOSS AT KODAK, Willard, liked to meet with the professional men and one woman during the lunch hour, playing cards in the conference room. Back in 1976, smoking was allowed in the workplace, and at least two of the men, including Willard, smoked their cigars during their game. Sometimes Willard would smoke one in his office, and it gagged me. However, it wasn't my place to complain.

For Willard's birthday, I thought it would be funny to bring in a cake with a cigar on top. My son's babysitter, Mamie, was skillful at creating cakes, so I asked her to make it for me.

The day of his birthday, I went to pick up the cake. When I saw it, I knew I was in trouble. The cigar stretched from one end of the sheet cake to the other – and it looked like, well...poop...or worse, a penis.

I had promised to bring in the dessert, so I swallowed my pride and headed to work with the cake.

As I carried it through the hallways, numerous people saw the cake and whispered and snickered behind my back. When I got to our department, I put the cake in the conference room, where Pat M. took one look at it and doubled over with laughter. He couldn't stop laughing all the way back to his office. My co-workers said, "I'm not eating that!" pointing to the cigar. "Ewww."

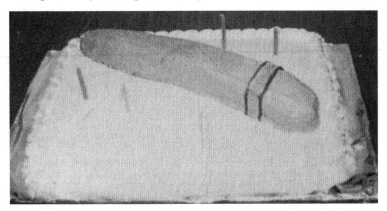

The Cigar Cake

When break time rolled around, everyone gathered for the celebration. I heard shrieking and howling from all the employees. I knew the cake was hideous, and I was trying to hide my embarrassment. The only thing I could do was laugh with them.

It was one of those moments that will forever be remembered by each and every person in my department. I still laugh about it.

A few years later, Pat M. was transferred to another job. The department honored him by having a luncheon at a fancy restaurant. When Pat got up to speak at the podium, Willard felt that the respectable thing to do was to put out his cigar. He doused it in his salad bowl which had a puddle of oil and vinegar at the bottom.

Back at the office, Willard got out the same cigar and relit it. The smell permeated the entire office and everyone demanded to know the source of the foul odor. Upon discovery, everyone ganged up on Willard and made him put it out. It was disgusting!

* * * * *

Oopsey!

KODAK'S PRESIDENT AND CEO WAS Walter Fallon at one point in my career. It was not unusual to see him in the hallways and elevators.

One day, I had to deliver some papers to another department, so I zipped out the double glass doors near my desk. At the elevators, Mr. Fallon was talking to Neil Murphy, Senior Vice President, Kodak, who headed film manufacturing at Kodak Park. I knew Neil from the Knights of Columbus, since my husband was a member. I said hello as they were getting on the elevator, but my high heel slipped on the vinyl floor causing me to twist my ankle and fall to the floor on my butt!!! To make matters worse, my full skirt flew up over my head, displaying my slip in full view.

I was never so embarrassed.

I gathered myself and got up, as their elevator door closed.

A week later I ran into Neil at the Knights of Columbus, where Jeff was the current Deputy Grand Knight. Neil pulled me aside and asked if I was okay after my fall. I said I was just embarrassed.

"Do you know what Walt Fallon said?" he asked me.

I shook my head no.

"He said, 'Nice legs!'"

I felt a little better after that.

* * * * *

STC Convention in D.C.

MY CO-WORKER AND FRIEND, Mary-Helen Maginn, and I were chosen from our Kodak Publications department to attend a Society for Technical Communication (STC) convention in Washington, D.C.

We flew down together and registered at the Courtyard by Marriott/Washington DC, Dupont Circle, across the street from the Hilton where President Reagan was shot in 1981.

As we went up to the check-in desk, the lady asked, "Are you a couple? Would you like a room together?" We laughed about the presumption and said no, separate rooms, please.

The next day we attended our lectures in the morning, but had the afternoon free. We decided to go to the National Zoo. We hailed a taxi outside of our hotel.

We jumped in the cab and I said, "National Zoo, please."

One minute later he dropped us off at the gate. It was just down the street! Haha! We had a good laugh about that and saved money by walking a couple of blocks back to the hotel afterwards.

Starlings

WE OCCASIONALLY HAD STARLINGS in our basement on Fairview Court. I'm not sure how they got in—perhaps through the chimney—but I was always on the lookout when I went to do my laundry.

Fairview Court, Greece, NY

My 8-year-old son Eric had a plastic Halloween pumpkin filled with Fisher Price people and cars that was kept in the basement and, once, when he went to play with the toys, he found a dead starling in the pumpkin. *Ewww.* I had to thoroughly wash everything.

Early one summer evening, while my husband Jeff was attending a Knights of Columbus meeting, I opened the basement door and a starling flew up the stairs and into the kitchen. I let out a yell, mainly because it startled me. Eric came running from his bedroom.

I thought that, if I could get the bird to fly through the kitchen door to our breezeway, I could open the two breezeway doors and it would find its way out.

"Eric, go grab a sheet so the bird doesn't fly into the living room," I ordered.

He got a sheet and I showed him how to hold his arms up and block the doorway while standing on a kitchen chair.

Eric held the sheet up to the two corners of the doorway—except that it drooped a little in the middle. That was enough for the starling to hop onto the sheet.

Eric started screaming because the bird was now close to his face. Instead of flying away, the starling jumped onto the top of his head! Eric was really screaming now. And he was still holding up the sheet. Obviously, there was no need to hold it up now since the bird was no longer in the kitchen.

I couldn't help it—I was laughing so hard, I couldn't stop. It was such a funny sight. Eric didn't think it was funny at all and kept screaming with the bird on his head.

Finally, it flew to an open shelving area on a half-wall. I opened the front door and the starling flew out, leaving behind lots of bird poop in my kitchen and living room that

I had to clean up. Eric didn't get pooped on, but I don't think he ever got over the incident.

ESP Classes

I STARTED TAKING EXTRA-Sensory Perception classes in 1977 in the Greece Adult Education program at Olympia High School, the year after I learned how to drive and bought my first car. On my first night, I met about 30 new people who had the same interests as I did. While waiting for class to begin, I picked up a copy of Edgar Cayce's book, *There Is a River*, and I was hooked.

Our instructor, Laura Smith, was wonderful and I signed up for several more classes over the years. But on this first night, one classmate, Ron B., who was also eager to learn about ESP and reincarnation, walked me out to my car. I led the way and stopped at the silver Chevy Nova in the lot and we talked about the class. It was quite chilly, being Fall, and I didn't want to stay outside for too long. At some point I looked at the Nova and saw a plaid interior. It wasn't my car!! I didn't want to tell this stranger that we weren't standing by the right car, but eventually everyone was leaving the parking lot and I had to admit my stupidity. He laughed his head off and never forgot it.

In one class, I was paired with an older lady and every "couple" in the class was given a compass. When she and I picked up our compass together, it spun around in reverse over and over! Everyone in the room was stunned and the teacher smiled and nodded with her approval. We had the power! I still get a chill down my spine when I think about it.

Ron and I also took a class from psychic and minister, Dan Chesbro, about 1986. Dan had met privately with the Pope and they discussed the Virgin Mary and her miraculous visitations. He also shared his visions with our class. Ron followed Dan and became a "Priest of Melchizedek," a worthy calling, committing to teach love and healing during his time on this earth.

Ron and I went to Dan's "spring equinox" sunset prayer ceremony on a hill overlooking Conesus Lake. I felt I was in the presence of God and among his apostles up on that hill. It was quite mystical. Even though it was June, I brought a heavy blanket because I knew how cold it can get in the Finger Lakes at night. As the group prayed with Dan, I noticed a girl in shorts and a sleeveless top and how badly she was shivering. I put my blanket over her shoulders and she almost cried with thanks. She said she couldn't have stood there a second longer, and then she felt the warm blanket... She said it was like a miracle. I was glad that I was there to help her.

Ron, his buddy Mitch, and I also signed up for a regression session (reincarnation) at a classmate's house. At the time, I was living on Seneca Parkway with the median in the middle of the road. Mitch was driving his van but drove down the eastbound side, while I lived on the westbound side. Ron walked across the median to my door and let me know where the van was. I had to carry a pillow and blanket across the median to Mitch's van. I can only wonder what the neighbors thought!!

I also took a T'ai Chi Ch'uan class for exercise, relaxation, meditation, and balance. I had issues with balance, but it helped me to relieve a lot of stress.

Going to these classes, learning meditation and so much about the power of ESP, and meeting amazing psychics, mediums, and seers, transformed me. It was as close to "serenity" as I could come.

Even though our lives moved on, Ron and I stayed connected over the years until his unexpected passing in 2017. His wife Gail gave me his crystals, books, runes, tarot cards, and a stone necklace and I have them displayed at home. I cried my eyes out at her generosity and how much they meant to me. He was a special soul—an "advanced" soul, and I think he's watching over me. During my last psychic reading he came through and left me messages, which I'll never forget. He told me that it was not my time to die yet; I had more to accomplish. Wow, he was so right.

Robbed!

IT WAS EASTER WEEK AND kids were off from school. That morning, I went into our "breezeway," the room that separated the house from the garage, and pushed a table all the way against the back door to the yard. I said to Jeff, "I'll know if anyone tries to break in if the table is moved."

Eric went to Mamie's for the day and for a few hours longer than usual because I had to go to a "going away" party for someone I worked with. That night, Jeff picked me up from the party and then we picked up Eric. As we exited the car and walked into the breezeway, I saw the table pushed away from the door!!

"Oh my God! Someone moved the table!" I exclaimed.

Jeff dryly replied, "Uh, look at the broken window in the door." You could see that they broke the window wide enough to put an arm through and open the bolt. Bastards!

We walked into the house, which was turned upside down. My dresser drawers were purposefully stacked in the living room, six high! Everything was ransacked. End-table doors were torn off their hinges. Speakers in the basement were kicked in. Jeff's wedding ring and his Gates-Chili High School ring were stolen, along with other jewelry, mine and his. My prescription for my back pain was gone. But they overlooked the $40 in cash on the kitchen table!

I called the police, who arrived quickly. The officer was surprised to see the HO-train setup in the living room and wanted to know if the burglars set it up! I told him no, that Jeff and Eric had been playing with it the night before. The officer went into my Chevy Nova in the garage and said that the glove compartment was open. They had obviously taken the set of keys on a hook inside the house, unlocked the car, looked through what little was in there, and stole a flashlight from the glove compartment.

The officer said, "This was the work of young kids, probably off from school."

I asked, "Why do you say that?"

"Because they stole the flashlight but not the car."

Aaah...

Soon the Crime Scene team arrived and fingerprinted the entire house. I had black fingerprint powder everywhere. What a mess!

They never caught the kids who did it, and they didn't expect to. Their fingerprints weren't on file.

The next day I called into work, asking if I could have a personal day to put my house back in order and to clean. Willard said I'd have to use vacation. I was bummed. On the second day, when I went back to work, I talked to my manager and he agreed to let me have a personal day.

Since the robbery, I've always looked for Jeff's high school ring, but never found it at any antique store or sale. I learned that jewelers often melt them down, so I don't think I'll ever come across it.

We bought a security system, but I wasn't comfortable staying in that house anymore. We put an offer in on an English Tudor on Seneca Parkway but someone else put in a higher bid and we lost out. I had convinced myself that I was meant to live there, so I couldn't understand how this happened. Two months later, the house was up for sale again, and this time we got it!

Life on
Seneca Parkway

Rochester, NY
1981-1999

.

Our English Tudor

RESIDING ON SENECA PARKWAY in the city of Rochester seemed extremely luxurious to us, compared to the 1,100-square-foot, 50s ranch we were used to living in. And there were surprises every time we turned around.

Seneca Parkway, Rochester, NY

The 4,600-square-foot 1926 English Tudor-style home was built like a fortress. It had a 12-inch-thick, full-brick exterior on the lower level and stucco above. When

Cornelius J. Schaeffer, owner of Central Laundry & Linen Supply, built the house for himself and his wife, he made sure that it was state-of-the-art (for the time) and every detail was perfect. He turned the house 90 degrees on the half-acre lot so that the main entrance faced east on the driveway instead of the street. In that way, he was able to maximize the square footage.

Later, the house was owned by the Gioia family of Gioia Macaroni.

In 1981, when we moved in, everything about the house was still original. At the arched entry was an Art Deco hanging light with a sailing ship on all four sides. Two granite scrolled sconces with white oak leaves graced either side of the entry. When you opened the heavy, curved, oak door, you walked into a small vestibule with a closet on the right and the original black-and-white octagon tile on the floor. You had to step up and open a leaded glass door to enter the foyer. A simple brass, hanging lamp lighted that area. The oak floor, bordered in mahogany, led to the formal living and dining rooms, and the honey-gold oak floor continued down a hallway and up the stairs.

The first thing you'd notice was a 7-layer crystal chandelier in the dining room; it was spectacular. There were two small crystal chandeliers in the 40-foot-long living room, and a whimsical butterscotch-crystal chandelier in the powder room. The flocked, green wallpaper in the entry and downstairs hall continued up the stairs. The butler's pantry (we used it as our breakfast room) had a brass chandelier and built-in poplar cabinets with leaded glass doors. It had the ONLY first-floor window overlooking a narrow view of the back yard, but you mostly saw the backside of the garage.

The kitchen was done entirely in blue-and-black ceramic tile with white floor-to-ceiling cabinetry. The Schaeffers could not have been very tall. I had to bend over the kitchen sink and always ended up with a backache. A multi-colored, flower chandelier hung in the center of the room. I'm sure the previous homeowners installed it. We didn't love it. One door led from the kitchen to the basement and also to the back door next to the attached garage. A secondary, back staircase led upstairs to the servants' quarters, and a swinging door led to the dining room, where there were servant buzzers on the wall and on the floor. (There was a buzzer in the living room as well.) The living room boasted two window seats (hiding huge radiators), leaded glass casement windows that opened inward, and built-in poplar bookcases on either side of a brick fireplace. The mantel extended over the bookcases, and poplar leaves, carved in plaster, decorated the facade. None of the woodwork on the first floor had been painted. Thank God.

The commode in the powder room had a short pull chain, a tank that filled from the top, and a teeny, tiny sink with separate faucets for hot and cold water.

A grand staircase took you to a wide landing and the second-floor hallway, which had two large, poplar linen closets. We took great pleasure in our 30-foot-long master bedroom and master bath (which we updated in 1981). A second bedroom and full bath were off the hallway, as well as a separate wing of the house that extended over the kitchen and the attached two-car garage. Off the long hallway in that wing were two bedrooms (most likely used by servants), a laundry chute, the back stairway to the kitchen, and the attic door.

We found the bedroom over the garage in poor condition. The interior walls were made of Homosote and there was only one electrical outlet. The inner wall of the room was well insulated with cork in case of a garage fire. (The servants could burn, but not the homeowners.) The room had two closets, one that extended almost the length of the bedroom for extra storage. (A great hiding place for kids! It actually had a light fixture back there.) This was the only room with cheap, pine flooring. The great thing about this room was that you could view the entire backyard and pool area from a great height. The bad thing was that the garage-door opener below the floor could jar you out of a sound sleep! It was also very cold or very hot, depending on the season. And sometimes raccoons climbed the ivy, relaxed on the wide window sill, and ate their "find," leaving the bones.

The other bedroom in that wing had wide casement windows that you could climb out of and onto a flat roof over the pantry. It sloped a bit to an efficient drain; efficient, that is, until the pussy willow tree dropped seedlings in the spring or leaves fell into the drain in autumn. Jeff had to climb out there, sometimes in deep water, and clear the drain. Twice we had ceiling leaks in the pantry, both times right AFTER we painted.

The stairs to the attic were creaky and chopped up, like someone had tried to modify them. The paneled attic was cavernous and had three small, attached rooms—a powder room, a walk-in cedar closet, and a room with a furnace, just for heating the third story. We discovered that there were several removable panels for access to the roof and chimney. We never saw the access itself because of the paneled ceiling. If the house hadn't been a Tudor, I would have imagined a widow's walk or a belfry. But, obviously, the roof access was there for the benefit of the construction workers.

The basement once had a coal bin that someone turned into a darkroom. Previous owners painted the walls blood red and added a mural. By the time we moved in, the walls were crumbling from moisture and the room had an eerie feel. The door to the room was swollen, heavy wood with a kid's *Beware* sign tacked on. You had to really tug to open the door, and it scraped on the cement floor. The light switch was funky. Switch it once, a red light came on; switch it twice, a normal light came on. When Jeff, Eric, and I first investigated the room, we found a bag of bones, which we assumed belonged to an animal, and a sword behind a large cabinet. The room was so creepy, we called it our Amityville Room.

The house had its own incinerator, not used in decades. Once, when a mourning dove fell down the incinerator chimney, I heard it trying to fly back up the chute to no avail. So, Eric and I went in the basement and opened the bottom of the incinerator. I gasped! There had to have been five feet of debris in there! The dove was no longer active and we feared it was dead. In any case, there was no way I was going to claw through the debris. We closed it up and never opened it again.

Outside we had an above-ground swimming pool with a deck that had been built into a small hillside. There was also a large grassy area, great for playing catch or bocce, and pavement for lounging and entertaining. A redwood stockade fence kept it private. Our two-car garage was not visible from the street and you had to open a large gate, drive through, and turn left into the garage between poles for the awning. For those reasons, we didn't use the garage much; we parked in the driveway by the main entrance.

When we purchased the home in 1981, one of the former owners was in federal prison in Kentucky for a few years. He was a judge who accepted a camera from a defendant and was convicted of bribery. Apparently, he also used ex-cons to do his yard work, and he had a continual feud with his next-door neighbor. We never met him, but our real estate agent told us that he and his wife went through the house when we put it up for sale in 1999. Our agent said he was very surprised and delighted to see what we had done. The son of the former neighbor also went through the house. He wanted to put in a bid for the house the day after we closed. Our agent had to say, "Sorry, Buddy. Too late." I guess he was really angry.

Once, around 1982, as I was shoveling snow, an older gentleman parked his car on the street and got out. His long, camel-colored wool coat dusted the top of the heavy snow as he walked up my driveway. He greeted me and tipped his fedora. I stopped what I was doing, feeling a bit embarrassed about my scruffy appearance.

"Hello!" he said cheerily. "Excuse me for interrupting. I once lived in this house with my uncle, Cornelius Schaeffer."

"Really!" I exclaimed.

"He built this house, you know."

"Yes. I know."

"What I remember most is the kitchen with the cabinets that reached to the ceiling."

I did not speak. My bones chilled. The kitchen had been pretty much destroyed by the previous inhabitants. Cabinets sawed in half. Paint on top of contact paper on top of glass and wood. Linoleum that rippled on the floor like an amusement park ride. Dirt and grease build-up behind the stove and sink.

"I'm wondering if it might be possible for me to see it again."

Oh, God! I had to think of some excuse. "Well, I'm sorry, but my husband is still sleeping." I was trying to justify my guilt. This man was a total stranger, after all.

He looked very disappointed. His eyes were downcast. I felt very guilty, but at the same time, I could not let him be horrified. That disappointment would be much greater and that's what he'd remember to his grave.

He thanked me for my time and left. I could have kicked myself for not getting his name and number. I thought that I could have at least invited him back after a week of intense scrubbing. But he was gone. And with him went many stories from the past. Perhaps even pictures.

How stupid I was.

When the kitchen walls were down to the studs, we found some mementos that Cornelius left for us. A silver spoon. A dairy bottle. I loved them and treasured them.

"Thank you, Cornelius, for giving me a little something from your era. I will leave something for future generations," I promised. Later, when we remodeled the master bath, I inserted a newspaper from the 1981 Gulf War and a note from me in the wall behind the toilet tissue dispenser.

I hoped that, in 25 years, someone would find them and know something about me.

Cats and Bats

THE FIRST THING I DID WHEN we moved into our new house was get a kitten. Patty Gekoski, my sister's friend, had a black kitten in a litter so she delivered it to Baumann Street where my parents still lived, and I brought it home. We named him Ming the Merciless (from Flash Gordon). Ming had a sweet personality and always cuddled with me. I trained him to use a harness and leash and we'd go on walks, usually not too far—about three houses or so in either direction.

A few houses down there was a young woman who often sat on the front steps with a guitar. Ming was immediately attracted to her and we'd go over there to listen to her play and visit. Her name was Anne Lise-Lotte, the daughter of Anni-Frid Lyngstad of ABBA, and she had come to Rochester to study. I later learned that she stayed in the Rochester area but died in a car crash in 1998 in Livonia, New York, where she lived with her husband.

We had a median that separated the east and west lanes of Seneca Parkway. Sometimes Ming (leashed) and I would go in the large median, especially when the cherry blossoms were in bloom. One evening at dusk, another cat appeared on the median and Ming (and I, following behind) chased the cat around several trees and, finally, it went up one of the cherry trees. If anyone had been looking out, they might not have seen my black cat in the fading light, but they would have seen me running willy-nilly around the trees and thought WTH.

One summer day, Ming decided to jump over our back fence into the next yard—except there was a Doberman Pinscher who was usually tied up there. I panicked when I saw Ming go over the fence, so I ran around the block to the house to bring him back home. I did catch him, but had to carry him along Lake Avenue, which freaked him out. By the time we got home, I was covered in claw scratches to my arms, chest, and abdomen and was so bloody, I had to shower and treat my wounds.

Sometimes Bob, the black-and-white cat from the Leathersich's house next door, would visit us and help himself to Ming's cat food. They'd chase each other all over the house, but never fought. Another neighbor gave her cat, Kimi Kitty, to me and she was with me for a few years until she developed cancer. I also brought home a stray tortoiseshell cat I named Goldilocks. I had her checked out at the vet and found that she was pregnant, so then I had 8 kittens, too. I gave all the kittens away, except one ginger cat, Sparky. Unfortunately, both Goldi and Sparky got sick and I had to put them down. I was back to just one cat, my Ming.

Ming was my constant companion for 16 years. He developed a thyroid problem so the vet put him on medication. The next day I had to go to an MP&AV conference in Kodak's Building 69 but Jeff was home because he was expecting our plumber to drain all the radiators and work on the boiler. Gary, the plumber, went to the main bathroom on the second floor and saw Ming sleeping on the cold tiles behind the toilet.

Gary exclaimed to Jeff, "That cat looks like he's dead!"

Jeff replied, "No, he always sleeps like that."

When Gary left, Jeff checked on Ming. He was dead. He broke the news to me when I got home. I cried, but laughed at the conversation with the plumber. He was too large to fit in a box, so we dug a hole behind our gazebo and buried him with his favorite toys. I put a large rock on top of the dirt. "Goodbye, Ming, my friend. You were the best cat ever and a true guardian. I'll never forget you."

* * * * *

There were other surprises in the house. Bats. Before we had the brick repointed, bats would squeeze through the broken mortar and get into the walls. You could hear them climbing inside the walls and squealing. From there, they would get through even the smallest of openings in the attic walls.

We had about 8 bats a year in the house. Jeff would leave them for me to discover—on the wallpaper, on the windows, flying across the room, crawling on their wings on the living room floor, dead inside a bucket of water and even inside one of my green-glass "lusters," which were on the mantle on either side of the fireplace. (It couldn't escape. Poor thing.)

I learned that if you contain a bat in one room and open the window at night, it will fly right out. I once told Marcia, "Sometimes I like to see a bat!"

Orphaned

SADLY, DAD PASSED away on December 4, 1982, in Florida, at the age of 67. Despite his proclaimed diet (in jest) of shredded wheat and whiskey, he had a heart attack and a massive stroke. The family flew down to Florida to be with him in his final hours in the hospital.

We left the hospital around midnight and went back to Mom's mobile home in Englewood. Around 5 a.m. the hospital called saying he had passed away. We all cried and had a drink, toasting to Dad. Mom asked who covered her up in bed during the night, but no one had. It must have been Dad! Then Patty saw the doorknob turning back and forth on their bedroom door! Everyone was in the living room! We all got the chills.

Mom turned on the news. We heard that actor Marty Feldman had died. There had also been a gas leak that caused a house to explode. The news reporter interviewed one of the occupants, a man perhaps in his 50s. He said, "I was sitting on the toilet, then heard this big explosion!" We laughed until we cried, again.

We had to fly Mom back to Rochester for the funeral service at OLPH. Her German Shepherd, Archie, had to be crated and sedated for the flight. The poor pup's crate was

SEARCHING FOR SERENITY IN MY CRAZY LIFE

THROWN by the baggage guy, as we watched. It's a wonder Archie survived!

On the first morning in Rochester, Mom awoke to hear the blender going in the kitchen at 6 a.m. She figured it was Dad telling her, "Everybody out of the pool!" his favorite expression to get everyone up and moving. The same day, I got a weird phone call with nothing but loud static. I think that was Dad, too.

The church was packed with mourners for the funeral Mass, and Msgr. Quinn remarked that he hadn't seen the church so full in years! Dad had made many friends over the years.

A few months later, we wanted to take Mom on a great trip to New England in the summer of 1983. It was decided that Jeff would drive Mom's car because it had more room and there were five of us—Mom, Patty, Jeff, Eric, and me.

On the first day we drove to Springfield, Massachusetts, and stayed overnight at the Holiday Inn. We woke up feeling excited about the new day and what we'd do and see. Jeff, Eric, and I met Mom and Patty in the Holiday Inn restaurant for breakfast.

In order for Eric to chew, he had to remove his dental appliance, used to push out his lower jaw and correct a bite problem. He carefully wrapped the appliance in a napkin and put it next to his place setting.

Feeling full after a hearty breakfast, we gathered our belongings and checked out of the hotel. Several miles down the road, Eric gasped, "Mom, I forgot my appliance!" In a panic and thinking about the $1,000 price tag, we returned to the hotel and scrambled to the restaurant, only to find a clean table with new place settings. I found our waitress and asked if she might have discovered his retainer. She said no. I asked what she might have done with his napkin and she said the kitchen staff would have dumped it into the trash.

The waitress led Eric and me into the kitchen, where we were directed to two heavy-duty trash bins, filled with breakfast remnants—pancakes, eggs, sausage, potatoes— the works. Ew. I had no choice; I had to go through them piece by piece. At the bottom of the second barrel, I found the appliance, still wrapped in the napkin. We rinsed it off and Eric popped it back in his mouth. Not a very pleasant thought, considering where it had been. And I really had to scrub up, for sure.

If that weren't enough, back out onto the road, the muffler fell off the car as we drove over a bump. Again, we had to turn around, find a muffler shop, and wait an hour until the car was fixed.

Eventually we made it to Mystic, CT, and Gloucester, MA, where we took in all the sites. In Gloucester, there was a shuttle that took us into town and picked us up. When we were finished shopping for the day, we walked toward the shuttle stop, and Mom was lagging behind. I yelled to her, "The shuttle's coming!" She walked as fast as she could, huffing and puffing. Unfortunately, no one realized at the time that Mom was in the beginning stages of lung cancer and she was not feeling well.

By the time we got to Gloucester, she had stopped eating altogether and only wanted a root beer float. That caused me great alarm. I knew something was terribly wrong.

Soon after that trip, she was diagnosed with the cancer, and I felt very, very guilty about rushing her to that stupid shuttle. We could have waited for the next one. I hope that she forgives me. But I'm glad that she got in one more vacation, though.

When Mom was dying of cancer at home, I felt that my sister Patty, her caregiver, needed a night out, and Mom agreed. She said she would be fine for a few hours.

We started out having dinner at The Pasta Villa on Ridge Road East in Irondequoit—a tiny place that has wonderful food. The owner and staff were extremely accommodating. Afterwards, Patty and I went to the Marriott Hotel on Ridge Road West in Greece where they had a live band playing. It wasn't quite time for the band, so we went to the bar for a drink. It was there that I ran into Roger B., who worked with me at Kodak.

Roger and his buddy asked us if we ever tried lobsters from the Genesee River. I knew he was teasing us, but Patty asked, "Really?" He went on to tell her how great they were, and Patty fell for it, hook, line, and sinker. Haha.

* * * * *

The last three days of Mom's life were spent at the hospital. On the third day, she took a turn for the worse. That day, I walked into her room alone and saw her comatose. Shocked, I cried out, "Mom!" Startled, she briefly sat up in bed, and looked straight ahead (not at me) to see who had called her name. Then she closed her eyes and went back down on her pillow. She was never conscious again. The rest of the family arrived and we all sat with her. At dinner time,

I told her, "We're going now. We'll be back after dinner." As soon as we left, she passed away, on May 18, 1984, at the age of 64. Damn cigarettes.

Marcia, Mickey, Patty and I lost both parents within 17 months. We were orphaned.

We went to the funeral home to make the arrangements and pick out the casket. Many people commented that they were shocked to read in her obituary that she was survived by both parents—and a grandson, Eric.

Before the viewing at the funeral home, Patty and I tried to find a pair of shoes in her closet without holes by the pinky toe. There weren't any, so we didn't deliver shoes to the undertaker.

I went to psychic Dan Chesbro a few weeks later and the first thing he said was, "Your mother is asking, 'Where are my shoes?'" Gasp! I told Patty, who freaked out and wanted to take a pair of shoes and bury them in her grave. We never did, though.

Patty, Marcia, her boyfriend Joe, Jeff, and I flew back to Florida to take care of everything in Mom's mobile home and get it ready for sale. We also went to Disney World for a couple of days. Patty told us that she met a guy named Tim McGraw who was really cute. She ended up marrying him in a ceremony in our house on Seneca Parkway!

On the plane trip back, out of Tampa, the wheels froze up on takeoff and the flight was suddenly aborted. The nose of the plane ended up sticking out over the edge of the Gulf of Mexico! Holy crap! Men in asbestos suits went up and down the aisle as the passengers sat there without protection in the smoky cabin. We had a 5-hour wait onboard with plenty of drinks but no bathroom! Then we were put up in a hotel for the night, where the five of us stayed in one room, with a cot and two beds. The next day we found out that we could have had two rooms. Sigh.

Patty continued to live on Baumann Street for another year. Most of the people from the old ethnic groups—the Poles, the Ukrainians, the Jews, and the Germans—were mostly gone. I had a dream that she found a large apartment near me in the Maplewood area, and in her search, she did, in fact, rent the second story of a house on Ridgeway Avenue, in back of Sacred Heart Cathedral.

As we cleaned out the house on Baumann, there were film processing chemicals in the basement. I was given instructions on how to dispose of them from Kodak, and I followed them closely. Patty, Jeff, Eric, and I took everything else out to the curb for pickup. On the same pickup day, the Gekoskis put an old, greasy stove to the curb that had been in their backyard for decades.

Apparently, the garbage truck picked up everything on our side, then picked up the stove. As they pulled ahead to the next house, there was an explosion in the back of the truck and the garbage man was blown out! They blamed the Gekoskis and their old stove, but we wondered if one of Dad's unknown chemicals might have been at the curb. We never knew for sure.

Interestingly, it happened to be Jeff's birthday, and Patty sent him a card that said, "Have a BLAST on your birthday!"

When Patty finally moved out, we said our farewells to the house we loved so much. The Spirit of the house on Baumann Street was no more.

The Prodigal Parrots

JEFF AND I WERE OUT AND about one evening when I suggested that we stop to see my brother Mickey, his wife Debbie, and my two-year-old niece Shannon. I preferred to give them notice, but we didn't have access to a phone. (Cell phones weren't popular yet.) It had been a while since we had seen little Shannon.

We pulled into their driveway on McNaughton Street and saw that their lights were on. In fact, ALL their lights were on, even the basement lights. *"Okay,"* I thought, *"Debbie needs to see where she's going."* Debbie was a diabetic who went temporarily blind the day after they brought baby Shannon home from the hospital in March 1984. For good reason, she was very depressed that she could not even see her baby. After partial eyesight returned, Debbie went through laser surgery to retain the vision she had. Nevertheless, she suffered permanent eye damage.

I rang the bell at the side door and before too long we saw Mickey shuffle down the three cellarway steps to the door. He was wearing his favorite blue velour shirt, and his natural afro was parted to the side, making it look a little lopsided. The family always teased him about "being adopted" because of his thick, frizzy dark brown hair, while the rest of us were redheads or blonde.

"Oh...this is not a good time..." Mickey warned us with a dour face. There was always drama in his life. He thrived on it. In fact, you never heard from him unless there was bad news of some sort. A few years later, he took his drama skills to the stage, performing in many Gilbert & Sullivan plays.

"Why? What's the matter?" I asked. I thought perhaps they were having an argument, but, hey, I was his sister and I felt like nurturing.

"Our parrots are missing!" The parrots were actually beautiful South American Nanday Conures, with green-and-yellow body plumage and black heads.

"Your parrots are missing?" I asked incredulously. Despite the situation and his warning, he ushered us into the house.

"We can't find them anywhere. We think they were stolen."

"Stolen? Who would steal two parrots?"

"Well, the meter reader was here today and he went into the basement. He probably heard the parrots squawking. Maybe he came up into the kitchen, saw that we had two expensive birds, and, you know, stuffed them under his coat." He demonstrated the last point.

I was trying hard to picture two upset parrots with very sharp beaks being tucked in a jacket next to very tender body parts. It just didn't make sense.

It *was* undoubtedly quiet in the house without those two birds squawking constantly—a real relief for both of us.

"The meter man left the cage?" I still had trouble believing this concept.

I noticed that Debbie was in the living room drying some tears and Shannon was upset because her parents were upset. They were still looking under cushions and sofas, probably for the third time.

Mickey continued, "The cage is still here, but the door was wide open. The parrots have never gotten out on their own before."

"Humph!" I thought. "Parrots are very clever birds."

Debbie and Shannon found their way into the kitchen through piles of debris. The whole house was torn up. "Hi, Ella," Debbie sniffled. "Sorry for the mess. I'm so upset. I can't believe someone would steal Spock and T'pring." The parrots were named after characters in *Star Trek*.

I gave Shannon a hug and a kiss. She was adorable with curly reddish-brown locks, a little turned-up nose, and big brown eyes.

Debbie was an eternal 60s flower child. Her long, blonde hair and her clothing gave her that forever-hippie appearance. Even though she was a chemist by trade, working at a pharmaceutical plant and later in Kodak's Research Labs, Debbie was very artistic. Several oil paintings and glass mosaics were propped up against the walls of their home.

Scanning Mickey's kitchen, I asked, "Are you SURE they're not in the house somewhere?" I had never seen such a mess. Their major kitchen appliances were in the middle of the room, and the contents of all the cupboards were stacked on the kitchen counters and table.

"We looked everywhere. We pulled out the stove and the refrigerator to make sure they weren't stuck behind them.

We even looked in the oven!" Mickey said, rubbing his tired face with his hand. You could tell they were exhausted.

"Could they have flown out when you came home and opened the door?"

"Their wings are clipped. They can fly down, but not up. That's why I'm going through the basement."

I pictured two green parrots hopping down the cellar steps to check out the basement. I wanted to giggle, but I figured Mickey and Debbie would be offended.

We wandered into the living room. A large ashtray filled with butts sat on a huge, round, cable reel that they used for a coffee table, and the room reeked of cigarette smoke. Even when they weren't upset, they smoked like fiends. I felt sorry for Shannon, living with intense second-hand smoke. I hoped she wouldn't smoke one day, especially after seeing my mom suffer and die from every cigarette-related disease—chronic bronchitis, asthma, emphysema, and lung cancer. It was a horrible way to go. Unfortunately, Mickey didn't learn from that experience.

The two maroon corduroy couches were pulled away from the walls, the large-screen TV was askew, and their belongings lay jumbled on the floor and tables.

Debbie's taste extended throughout the house—a funeral-parlor floor lamp, antiques of every kind, a reptile tank under a heat lamp for their lizard, and several plants (nothing suspicious that I could identify) under a fluorescent light. There was bird poop here and there that, obviously, Debbie couldn't see.

"How long have you been looking?" I inquired.

"Since we got home about 5 o'clock," Mickey said. It was now a little after 7 o'clock.

Debbie lit a cigarette. "Oh, Ella. I can't believe they're gone," she moaned while she puffed.

"They were so expensive, too," I added.

"Oh yeah." She took another drag on her cigarette. "When I first saw them, I knew I had to buy them for Mike."

She always called Mickey "Mike." Only relatives called him "Mickey," a nickname I'm sure he outgrew as soon as he attended ninth grade at Benjamin Franklin High School. He probably would have been pummeled with a name like "Mickey." When he was a baby, the family used to sing a ditty to the tune of the Mexican hat dance: *"Michael Lawrence, Michael Lawrence, lala lala la. Michael Lawrence, Michael Lawrence, la la lala lala la."* Anyway, it was comfortable for me to call him Mickey unless I called him at work.

The parrots were the first of many animal gifts Debbie bought "for Mike." One time, they had seven dogs—five Miniature Schnauzers, one Miniature Doberman Pinscher, and one Great Dane. She said Mike and Shannon would love them, but they were her babies. Mickey gave into all her whims; he had a problem saying no.

On occasion, if Debbie had surgery or they went camping, they would ask me to dog sit. I wasn't sure how I'd handle all seven dogs. I knew I couldn't handle seven leashes. And when the dogs had to do "their duty," they had to exit the side door, turn right, and go through the chain-link gated fence into the grassy backyard. I was afraid that they would all run in different directions and I'd be chasing them down the street. To stay in control, I tried letting just one dog out at a time. But the six remaining dogs cried and scratched at the cellar door and the outside dog refused to go in the backyard, even with my insistence. ALL of them had to go out at once; and when they did, they ran, barking and yapping, in a pack up the driveway to the backyard. It was a great relief to me that Debbie had trained them so well and that they trusted me.

Jeff and I weren't sure what to do about their parrots. Jeff would have preferred to go home and leave them with their dilemma. I believed the birds were still in the house. And something inside of me told me I could find them if I just thought like a parrot. Where would I go???

I turned to Debbie. "I might be able to find them using a dowsing rod," I offered.

"Oh brother," Jeff teased under his breath. "Here we go!"

Okay, so he didn't believe me, but I felt great confidence.

There was a glimmer of hope in Debbie's eyes. "Really?" she asked, her curiosity peaked.

"A dowsing rod? Isn't that for finding water?" Mickey asked.

"Not necessarily." I explained. "You just have to ask the right questions."

"Okee, dokee." Mickey had great patience for out-of-the-box thinking. After all, he lived with Debbie who always conjured up natural remedies and what-not. "But doesn't a dowsing rod have to be made from hazelwood or something?"

"I can make one out of a bobby pin. Debbie, do you have one?"

"Sure. Let me go get one." She went upstairs.

While she was gone, I drew a rough sketch of their first floor on a piece of scrap paper. When Debbie returned with the large bobby pin, I bent it so that it forked out like a dowsing rod. I asked everyone to leave me alone in the kitchen for a few minutes.

I closed my eyes and prayed, "Let the white light surround me. I pray for the highest and the best...Where are Mickey's parrots?" When I was ready, I lightly held my dowsing rod in my fingers, moving it over the sketch from room to room. Whenever I held it over the area by the TV, my fingers started to tingle. It took me off guard; I even surprised myself. The sensation wasn't quite *over* the TV, just *next to* it. I repeated it over and over and always got the same reaction.

Excited, I called to Mickey, "Get me a flashlight, quick!" My heart was beating loudly and I was afraid that my intuition would be wrong. I hoped it wouldn't be.

Mickey handed me a black flashlight that was nearby. I walked into the living room where everyone was gathered and surprisingly silent. I turned on the flashlight and picked up the square floor fan sitting next to the TV.

"I found your birds," I said bluntly. I had goosebumps all over.

Everyone gasped.

"Are they dead?" asked Debbie, dreading my reply.

"Nope!" I turned the floor fan around to reveal two terrified parrots clinging to the metal grid of the fan.

"Oh my God!" Mickey and Debbie screamed in unison.

Mickey was totally astonished. "They were *there* all this time???? You don't know how many times I moved that fan and they didn't even squawk!"

"How did you know they were there?" Debbie asked while she carefully put each one in their cage.

"I had to think like a parrot. They thought the metal fan was their cage!"

We all started laughing. Mickey said he couldn't wait to tell everybody at work how his sister found his prodigal parrots!

Shawcross

FOR A FEW MORNINGS in a row in 1990, I saw a 4-door sedan parked on the corner of Seneca Parkway near Lake Avenue where I'd catch my bus. There was a fat, old man sitting inside. After the third morning, I was angry and I wanted to tell him to get the hell off of my street. But I didn't dare. And that was a smart thing.

I looked like a "bag lady" going to the bus at 6 a.m.— raincoat, dress, athletic shoes, a striped tote bag loaded with dress shoes, a breakfast bagel, a bag of cat kibble (you never know when you'll meet a hungry cat), and work papers that I carried home to review each night.

I never looked this man in the eye; I just walked to the bus stop and watched for the bus. I could see the bus as it stopped at Kodak Park, so I knew when it was approaching. On those three mornings, it couldn't come soon enough. The guy made me very nervous.

That night on the local news, I heard that they caught serial killer Arthur Shawcross, who had been hanging around Salmon Creek and Northampton Park on Route 31 in Brockport, New York, where he had dumped a body a few days before. When the news program showed a picture of his car (actually his girlfriend's car), I almost fainted. It was the same car that I had seen at the corner of my street when I caught the bus! That really shook me to the core.

Relieved that he was finally caught and would no longer be sitting by my bus stop, I continued to take the bus. However, a series of incidents made me decide to drive the seven miles down Lake Avenue to the office.

There was another short, fat, old man who drove an orange Ford Pinto (I took down his license plate number) who stopped while I was waiting for the bus, rolled down his window, and said, "I'll give you $50 if I can rub your stocking." Ewww. I ignored him and walked away. When I told Jeff that evening, he said I should have thrown my panty hose in his window, grabbed the $50, and run away. Yeah, very funny, Jeff.

One cold, wintry morning, there was a 20-something guy walking south on the sidewalk toward my bus stop. He said someone just robbed him and took his jacket. He was shivering. He asked me if I could give him some money. I told him I only had $5 for my lunch, so he moved on. He ended up coming back and asking me if I wanted to go on a date sometime. Haha! I told him that I was old enough to be his mother.

Then there were two very drunk African-American ladies who were carrying a bottle of booze and taking turns drinking from it. They were walking in the middle of the bus lane. When they got close to me, they got in my personal space and asked me if I wanted a swig. I said no thanks. Then my bus approached. They both jumped out in front of the bus!! Luckily, he stopped in time. I decided then and there that I had enough. It was time to drive to work.

There were other "close encounters" with crime when I lived on Seneca Parkway. When we had two pussywillow trees, someone climbed one of them and tried to break in through one of the small (sealed) windows next to the chimney. We noticed it and immediately resealed the window. That night he came back and made another unsuccessful attempt. We saw his fingerprints in the putty, and called the police. This time we cut down the pussywillow trees, too.

Early one morning I took Ming the Merciless out for a walk on his leash. An older man in a trench coat (first clue) was coming down the sidewalk. As he approached, he flashed me. Yup, the "full Monty." I screamed, "Jefffff!" The man ran toward Dewey Avenue.

And one night while we were watching TV, we heard sirens getting closer and closer. Then flashing lights were circling inside our living room. We looked out and were warned by police to get away from the windows. There were at least 5 police cruisers on our lawn with their headlights facing our house!! Apparently, there was a guy with a gun hiding in our shrubs! After that instance, we had the shrubs removed and we re-landscaped.

The 1991 Ice Storm

THERE ISN'T ONE ROCHESTER, NY, resident who lived here in 1991, who doesn't remember our infamous ice storm on March 4th. The weather report that Sunday did mention that ice was a possibility, but no one foresaw the storm that shut down the city and miles around for two weeks.

It was a normal Sunday for us. We needed a small kitchen table and a couple of chairs to put in our butler's pantry that we used as a breakfast nook. We had recently remodeled the kitchen with Wood Mode light cherry cabinetry and there was no longer room for a table. We did have a formal dining room, but we used it only for special occasions. We took a drive to Service Merchandiser's on Ridge Road West and found a maple table with two Windsor chairs with black trim. The store was one of those places where you'd place an order at a desk and the product would come boxed, rolling down a series of rollers where the customer would pick it up and take it home, unassembled.

That evening we spent putting the very sturdy table together. After an hour or so and a few curse words, Jeff had it assembled.

We went to bed early since we had to get up for work the next day.

The next morning Jeff got up and showered and I followed shortly thereafter. Nothing seemed different. I could hear Jeff scraping his windshield as I got ready to leave the house.

I stepped outside into a winter wonderland. I was speechless. There was ice everywhere—on the steps, on the driveway, on the trees, on the houses, and on the wires. I could hear it crackling. I had to be very careful walking four houses to the bus stop on Lake Avenue. When I got to the stop, I looked around in astonishment. There were broken tree branches everywhere, and wires were hanging very low. I tried to keep away from the tree looming above the sidewalk and hoped a large limb would not come crashing down on me. It was still sleeting and the icy rain hit my face and uncovered calves like little needles. I waited for the bus for almost 45 minutes. By the time the bus arrived, all of my exposed hair was covered in ice. There were only a half dozen people on the bus; normally it would be packed like sardines.

The ride down Lake Avenue was utterly amazing. The ice was beautiful but devastating. I couldn't believe how many trees and branches were down. We'd hear a large crack and another branch would come crashing down, splintering the ice like glass. Cars had to avoid the branches in the road. It was a dangerous place to be.

I got into work and took the elevator up to the 3rd floor. The office was dark and chilly. No one was there. I turned on the lights at the switch box. After taking off my wet jacket, I hung it over a chair to dry. The phone in our manager's office started to ring. I went over to answer it—one of the writers was taking the day off because she lost power.

Over the next two hours, I answered the manager's phone from almost everyone in the department. I think I was the only one who was there working.

At 10 a.m., the phones finally ceased and I decided to go home. There was no point in staying. The sleet had stopped, and the bus arrived after a short wait. On the ten-minute ride home, it was like a ghost town. No one was out and about.

I called my neighbor Nicki Leathersich to see if she and her family were okay.

"Ella, too bad about your pool."

"My pool?" I asked, puzzled. "What do you mean?"

She started laughing. "You mean you didn't hear the tree in the backyard crashing down into your pool about 6:30 this morning?"

"Oh my God, no!"

"We heard this loud crack and then a boom that shook the entire house. We looked out the window and saw that the black walnut tree had broken in half and had fallen into your pool. I can't believe you didn't hear it!!"

"I was probably in the shower at that time. And the walls of our house are about 12 inches thick. It's practically soundproof."

Nicki also told me that she had spoken to our other neighbor Julie Boland. And Julie had spoken to her neighbor whose son was a lineman. He apparently saved us from a power outage by climbing up the utility pole in the back yard and securing the power line. Our side of the street never lost power; the people across the road were in the dark. I don't think they got power back for almost two weeks.

1991 Ice Storm

I called my brother and sisters. Mickey and Patty had both lost power, but they were going to hunker down and weather it out. Marcia was okay.

I went out to see the damaged pool and took some pictures of the ice in my yard. I could hear the sound of chain saws. It's a sound that I would hear every daylight hour for the next two weeks, well after the ice had melted and the sun had come out. In one night, Rochester lost about 80% of its trees.

As a result of our damaged pool, we decided it wasn't worth fixing. The lining was gone.

We ended up with a deep, 16-foot circular hole in the ground because the pool was built into a slope. We decided to replace the pool with a gazebo—something I had always wanted, and it would go well in our Victorian neighborhood.

We drove down to PA and found a very large outbuilding manufacturer called Rick's Sheds. We picked out a gazebo and had it custom-built and made arrangements for them to drive it up to Rochester on a flatbed truck. On its first attempt, the truck broke down and we had to reschedule the delivery. The second attempt was a success. A friend of mine from work, Ed Blasko, called me to say he had seen a truck with a gazebo on it going down the expressway. It was mine!

One of the local printers I worked with (Lou C.) asked if he could come to our house and watch it being installed. I said sure! Lou had a glass of wine while I took pictures of the gazebo being slid into place. It was on skids so it wasn't directly on the ground.

Gazebo

143

We built up two sides with a rock wall, added a pebble path from the driveway to the gazebo, and landscaped all around.

I missed not being able to lounge on an air mattress in the pool, but the gazebo gave me many years of enjoyment. I could never forget that it all started with the '91 ice storm.

Garden Visitors

WITH MY HANDS ON MY HIPS, I stood on the gravel path over the multi-level, fiberglass aviary pond I had received for Mother's Day. I loved my gift, but on this night, it presented some challenges. The pump was gasping and the water wasn't cascading. The pond was obviously not level. And it was filthy.

Nightly visitors drank from it and washed their paws, leaving muddy water and muddy prints behind. It didn't bother me that nighttime animals found this oasis in the stifling heat of a summer's night. What bothered me was that, every time I dumped the water out, it washed away some dirt underneath. The water would run down the slope of my terraced garden and onto the gravel path beside my gazebo. When I repositioned the pond, it took a great deal of effort to make it level.

It was going to be dark in an hour or so, but I still had time to clean the pond and level the foundation. Hopefully, I could sit and enjoy the birds for a while, too. I unplugged the pump from the outlet at the base of my gazebo, dumped the water, disassembled and removed the pond. Using some flat stones, I tried to level the pond. I knew, at best, it was a very temporary fix. I had to come up with a better solution. I just needed time to think.

I filled a little seed tray near the cavity for the pond and I sat down into a deep-cushioned wicker chair in the gazebo. Before long, a few English sparrows showed up, kicking the seed to the ground. I watched as they chased away two house finches before they, themselves, flew away. I glanced towards the house and, suddenly, I knew what to do about the pond.

There, against the house, was a large, white concrete paver. Jeff had purchased two for the entrance to the gazebo, but had only used one. I got up from my chair, determined to level my pond—tonight.

I knew the concrete paver would be heavy, so I bent my knees before trying to pick it up. I was shocked that I could barely lift a corner of it off the ground, much less carry it across the driveway, down the gravel path, around the gazebo, lift it above the stone garden wall and into the terraced slope. I thought about asking Jeff for help, but I knew he was working on the computer and wouldn't like being disturbed. I imagined he would ask, "Why can't we do this on the weekend?" I didn't want to wait. I was too impatient and excited with my find.

I thought I could push the paver with my foot. It didn't budge.

I was perplexed, but I looked inside the garage for a solution. Behind a pallet laden with bags of fertilizer, potting soil, and peat moss was a flat, square dolly. *"That's it!"* I thought. The only problem was that I would have to move the pallet to get to the dolly. I started removing the bags, one by one. When I got to the fertilizer, the bag broke and the fertilizer spilled all over the garage floor. Drats! I didn't need a problem like this and Jeff would not be pleased. I imagined what he would say and it wasn't pretty.

Not to be discouraged, I lined a trash can with a plastic bag, moved the pallet out of the way, and swept up all the fertilizer into the bag. My back was starting to ache and night was quickly approaching, but I didn't want to stop now. I was so close.

With the mess cleaned up and the dolly in my hands, I went back to the paver. I still had to lift it onto the dolly. My first attempt sent the dolly rolling across the driveway without the paver. The second time, I braced the dolly against the house so it couldn't go anywhere. I picked up a corner of the paver and pushed it onto the dolly. *"So far so good,"* I thought. I got the second corner on, too. Then I was able to push the entire paver onto it. Eureka! Success! The dolly was ready to go.

I rolled the dolly with the paver to the edge of the garden, where a concrete curb forced me to stop. A robin was singing his evening song from the top of the cherry tree. I waited for a moment to revel in it and to stretch my back. *"Argh!"* This was not easy work for a 50-year-old woman! When the robin flew to the next yard, I once again focused on the job at hand.

My next dilemma was how to get the paver down the terraced slope. I couldn't use the dolly. I decided to place the paver upright on the mulch and "roll it" down the hill. After my first "roll," it flopped flat to the ground. *Boom!* "Okay," I said aloud, "I only need to do this three more times and, if I do it right, it will drop right into the hole for my pond."

It took all of my strength to pick up and flop the paver each time. Flop. *Boom!* Flop. *Boom!* Flop. *Boom!* To my amazement, the paver fell perfectly into place! I stood up with satisfaction, but very slowly because my back was truly aching.

Then, out of the corner of my eye, I saw a slight movement near my feet. A little rustle of the holly bushes. Black fur low to the ground. I felt confused because my black cat Ming was inside the house. I froze. I don't think I ever felt horror and curiosity at the same time, but there, waddling out of the bushes came three adorable baby skunks. They were obviously looking for the birdseed that was scattered on the ground and for a cool drink of water from the pond that lay disassembled on the gravel path.

I backed up slowly on the terraced garden and moved a few inches toward our stockade fence, trying not to trip on the plantings. I didn't want to be threatening; and I certainly didn't want to be sprayed. When I saw Momma skunk poking her face out of the bush behind the babies, I became terrified. I should have known she wouldn't be far behind them. I was sure that I posed a threat to her babies and wondered if she could sense my fear. I continued backing up very slowly until I got to the driveway, then I took off like lightning toward the garage. I glanced behind me. To my shock, the three little ones were following me! They were all in a row, their little feet carrying them as fast as they could. I wondered, *"Are they confusing me with their Momma— their provider of food and water?"*

I ran into the garage and hit the garage-door opener. The sound of the garage door closing startled the baby skunks and they stopped in their tracks. It seemed to take forever for the garage door to close, but I watched the babies as they ran back to Momma, who was still peering from the bushes.

It was probably the last time they trusted a human. But I thanked Momma skunk for trusting me temporarily. I thought, *"If it weren't for her trust, I probably would be taking a tomato-juice bath about now."*

I waited until the next day to finish my project, but the paver was the perfect solution! The pond was level, the water cascaded properly, and I didn't have to worry about washing away the foundation. The sound of moving water continued to draw multitudes of birds and other wildlife that came to quench their thirst, dip their heads, and splash around. I could sit in the gazebo, listen to the gurgle of the waterfalls, and enjoy the birds for hours on end. And my encounter with the skunks? Well, in a way, they gave their special blessing to my pond, and I never complained about the muddy footprints again.

Diversity Training

IN 1999, KODAK MANAGEMENT required all of us to take several hours of diversity training and it would be reflected in our Performance Appraisals the following January.

There were many options to consider. For example, I could have attended a meeting of the Women's Forum of Kodak Employees. Or I could have met with a leader of Network North Star, which promoted and enhanced the career potential of African-American employees through mentoring, educational programs, and seminars. Or I could have gone to a luncheon seminar with the Asia-Pacific Exchange group, which helped Asian and Pacific Islander heritage employees to attain career goals. But these options all seemed too common. I wanted to do something really different, that no other employee would do.

My co-worker and cubicle neighbor, Jean Wallace, felt the same way. One day she came to me with a newspaper article. It read, "The Greater Rochester Area Branch of the American Association of University Women will be visiting the Islamic Center of Rochester, 727 Westfall Road, Rochester, NY at 10 a.m. on Saturday, May 12, 1999. Christianity and Islam: A Dialogue Between Perspectives, and The Bible and the Quran will be discussed. Call the AAUW to attend."

I got excited. No one else in our department would be going to this discussion. It was perfect. Jean made the call and we were in.

One of the requirements for the mosque was that we had to cover our hair, and we had the perfect solution. A printer friend of ours, Ben H., had just returned from India and had presented each of us with a long, beautiful Indian scarf. Mine was pink and Jean's was green.

The morning of our diversity training, I went to Jean's house and we drove to the mosque together. We got there a little early but we had to drape ourselves in the scarves. They were much longer than we expected, and after several ways of wrapping it around our head and shoulders, we finally got them the way we wanted. We took one look at each other and we burst out into hysterics! We couldn't stop laughing, I gasped for breath, and I almost peed my pants.

As we saw more of the University Women arrive, we got out of our car. We noticed that everyone was staring at us and we thought that we were just strangers to them. Eventually, a female Muslim came to greet us and introduced herself. We were required to remove our shoes at the door. One of the University ladies had to use the restroom and was told that she could put her shoes back on. Another lady approached us and asked me, "Why was she allowed to wear her shoes in the restroom?" It was apparent that she thought we were Muslim. I casually replied, "It's a New York State health law." Jean and I exchanged looks.

We were led inside the mosque and were totally respectful. We were told that the Muslim men and boys were

151

allowed to use the space upfront for prayer and that they were hip-to-hip with each other when they knelt. The women were not allowed upfront, but were to remain in the rear. Ritual prayer is called Salat, made five times a day on a prayer rug while facing Mecca, which in the U.S. is east-southeast. According to Muslim beliefs, the prayer times were taught by Allah to Muhammad and represent a connection to the Creator.

A stunningly beautiful Muslim woman came forth and I'm sure we all gasped at her beauty. She could have been a model, if they allowed such things. She made comparisons between the Bible and Quran, stating that we believe much the same in the Old Testament. But the New Testament was where the common beliefs stop. They believe Jesus was (just) a prophet and is not God.

There were many cultural differences as well. We were told that Muslims only use cash. No credit, even to buy a house. She also informed us most Muslims are not radical as some in the Mideast. There were several questions posed and answered, focused mainly on the Gulf War and terrorists, and it seemed that these Muslims were quite peaceful and moderate and happy to be in America.

After about an hour, we were thanked for coming and we thanked them for the informative session. We learned a lot. The head of the University Women invited us for lunch at the King and I Thai Restaurant, to which Jean and I heartily agreed.

The group sat in the restaurant's back room and tasted many Thai dishes, passed around family style. You could smell basil everywhere. My favorite dish was the sweet and sour fish. We introduced ourselves and gave the ladies a little background as to why we attended. We were asked to join their group and receive their newsletter (although I never did). The ladies were delightful and funny and we had the best time!

The Pond

IT WAS A SULTRY JULY morning and I was on vacation from work. The sun was shining in a perfectly blue sky and I hated to leave the beauty and serenity of my yard with chirping birds fluttering in and out of my aviary pond. I was off to spend a day with Patty and her two sons, Ryan and Alex, and perhaps catch a glimpse of some bluebirds.

Her town, Victor, is about a half hour away from Seneca Parkway, most of it expressway. The countryside is picturesque and clean, deer abound on its rolling hills, and birds of every color and song make their homes there. It's no surprise that it's a favorite of the rich. Unfortunately, Victor is a victim of urban sprawl. The wealthy are destroying the natural beauty and habitat that they came to enjoy. Gargantuan houses cut into many of the hills, so close to each other that they clog up the countryside. You have to wonder if Victor will someday be a suburban slum and the rich will keep moving deeper and deeper into the country, making the same mistake with the next town.

Luckily, Patty's tract was hidden in a valley surrounded by woods and hills, so it didn't seem as intrusive. Her road wound down the valley, continued past her house and up the next hill. That's where the housing construction ended,

154

so far. On this day, the sound of drills and nail guns disturbed the peace of the halcyon day, but no one seemed to notice except me.

Ryan and Alex just woke up and they were lounging as they watched a cartoon on TV. Alex wanted to curl up to Patty with his blanket. He liked to play with his ear as he sucked his thumb and rubbed the blanket on his cheek.

"He needs to wake up gradually," Patty told me. "He's my cuddle-bunny." She stroked his hair and face and kissed him on the head. His long black eyelashes and cherub features gave him the look of an angel. *"Someday he's going to be a lady-killer,"* I thought.

Patty made a promise for breakfast and I yearned for eggs, toast, and coffee. What I got was a day-old doughnut. Haha. But the coffee was good and it perked me up. Patty sent the boys upstairs to get dressed. A little while later, they came down in mismatched clothing, but it was what they chose.

"Alex, put on your shoes and socks!" Patty said for the tenth time. "We're going for a walk."

"Why?" he asked.

"Because Aunt Ella wants to see the pond." I saw a flicker of excitement in Alex's eyes.

Patty turned to me. "We saw a heron in the pond the other day."

I looked out the sliding glass door that opened onto her second-story deck. The tract's drainage pond was just a house or two away, sitting among reeds and swaying grasses. From her last comment, it was clear that she was going to take me to the drainage pond instead of the one I so desperately wanted to see.

"I was hoping you could take me to the *other* pond." I hoped she understood.

"Oh...the one in the meadow!"

"Yeah, I'd love to see it."

When Patty moved into her new house, she and the boys discovered the pond quite by accident. They were exploring the area when she spotted it on top of the hill, hidden from all the houses.

"Okay," she agreed. "Come on, guys. Let's get a move on!"

Alex was already sweating from a tussle with his brother.

"Can I take my bike?" Ryan asked.

"How are you going to get a bike up there?" Patty asked. "You can ride it later."

At last, the four of us were on our way. The sun was beating down on us and I was glad Patty had offered sunscreen before we left.

We wandered around the construction site of one of the new houses. We peered in a window and said hi to one of the workers. Patty told me about the time, just after they moved in, when Tim confronted a construction worker inside their house! Tim angrily asked, "What the hell are you doing here?"

They guy played dumb. "Oh, I didn't think anyone moved in here yet."

Tim responded, "So that's why there's a car in the garage and furnishings in the house." He threw the guy out and called the construction company. They informed him that there had been items stolen from homes in their tract recently and they would take care of this matter quickly.

Patty, the kids, and I continued walking in the field around the new house. Patty stopped dead. "Look!" she cried. "A nest!"

There on the gravel, in between patches of grass, were two spotted killdeer eggs. We had almost stepped on them. Alex and Ryan studied the nest closely as Patty explained to them how the bird camouflaged its eggs among the stones so predators couldn't see them.

I thought, *"What a good mom!"* I was sorry that Eric and I didn't have access to these surroundings as he grew up.

The house across from Patty's was also under construction. "When they cleared the land," she lamented, "baby killdeer were crying from their nest. The mother was screaming. Suddenly there was silence. The bulldozer covered up the nest with dirt." My stomach turned. I wished she hadn't told me. Construction shows no mercy.

Patty went on, "The house next door to it has had all kinds of flooding problems. They're suing the builder."

I looked at the steep slope that ended at the back door of the house. *"I wouldn't want to have that hill in my backyard!"* I thought.

"The hill is manmade and when the snow melted this spring, the water rushed down, washing away their landscaping and running right into the house. They replanted everything and it happened again! So now they're suing."

"Why did he put the hill there in the first place?"

"I think it was the excess dirt from the tract. He needs to re-grade the hill, or something."

I was picturing the mess and feeling their frustration. And I couldn't imagine how much money they put into their landscaping, especially after building such a magnificent house.

Patty pointed to the roof of another half-million-dollar house. "Look at that roof."

"Eww! There's bird poop all over it!"

"The pigeons always flock there. I don't know why. They've tried everything; they can't keep them off."

Next, Patty pointed to a steep driveway on the left. "We can cut through the yard here."

I hesitated. "The neighbors won't care that we're cutting through their yard?"

"No, it's alright. We do it all the time. They know me and I don't think they're home anyway."

My heart was pounding by the time we reached the top of the driveway! *Pant, pant!*

Alex cried, "Mommy! Carry me!" She scooped him up, while Ryan ran ahead.

We finally reached the top of the hill. I gasped with delight! There in front of us was a wide meadow with wildflowers and tall grasses, dotted with an occasional fruit tree. I imagined that an orchard once flourished here.

"A bobolink!" I cried, pointing to the very top of a lone apple tree. We listened to it sing.

"No. I don't think that's a bobolink." Patty squinted to see the bird better.

"Sure it is. See the bright yellow nape and the white patch near the tail?" We crept closer, trying to get a better look at him.

I stumbled briefly in a furrow, but quickly recovered my balance. My ankle throbbed a little and sweat was running down my neck. The bobolink continued his song. It was beautiful. I thought I was in heaven. We inched closer. Patty put Alex down. The bobolink spotted us and stopped singing. Eventually, we were too close and he flew off to the next tree.

"There's the pond!" Patty pointed it out to me.

My eyes scanned the landscape until I spotted the pond, which blended into the background. I increased my gait, anxious to get a good look, but cautious of ruts hidden in the grass. The pond was about 90 feet long and 60 feet wide. The water sparkled in the bright sun. I was surprised to see a dock, which stretched several yards into the pond. We ran out there, giggling like children.

"Oh my God! It's beautiful! I could stay here forever!" I cried.

There was no breeze to cool us, but the water calmed us. Patty and I both let out a big sigh.

"Could we sit here for a while?" I asked as salty sweat rolled into my eyes.

"Sure."

I sat on the dock, trying to absorb the beauty of the scene so that it stayed with me forever. There was a willow tree in the corner dipping its fronds into the water. The water was fairly deep and, no doubt, great for swimming or fishing. The pond seemed surreal, like part of a dream, and I didn't want to wake up.

Alex knelt on the rough planks. "Ouch!" he yelled. He held his hand up to reveal a nasty sliver. Tears started welling up in his eyes.

"It's okay, Alex," I said comfortingly. "We'll get it out with tweezers when we get back to the house and it'll be gone in a jiffy!"

Fear. Pure fear appeared on Alex's face. And Ryan's too.

Patty gasped. She whispered, "Never tell them 'tweezers.' They can already feel the pain." Alex was holding back the tears. Removing the sliver with tweezers was worse than death, apparently.

I immediately regretted saying the "T" word. Of course, little kids are terrified by them. Soaking it out was the better method anyway.

I knew that our adventure was already over, and my dream world disappeared in a puff of smoke.

"We need to go back," Patty said. I turned to take one more look at the pond. I wished that I had brought my camera. (For some reason, Kodak employees never remember their cameras!)

For a few short minutes I had been transported to another era without expressways and huge housing tracts. A pastoral scene from the early 1900s. Pure serenity. I was terribly saddened to leave that place. I wanted to capture it forever in my mind. I thought, *"I'll never see this pond again."*

* * * * *

Two years later, Patty's tract was completed and other tracts were springing up around it. Jeff and I drove up to the cul-de-sac at the top of the highest hill. I gasped in horror. There was the little pond, now without a dock and the beautiful willow, surrounded by three megalithic houses. Tears filled my eyes. *"How could they do that?"* I thought. No more serenity. No meadow, no bobolinks; just house upon house. And the little pond, once so sweetly sparkling in the sun, was looking pitifully lonely, like the drainage pond in Patty's backyard. It was the saddest moment for me in many years.

Jeff and I drove away and this time I didn't look back.

Ratfinger

ANOTHER UNEVENTFUL DAY PASSED and it was time for bed. I dozed off on the love seat a few times during a primetime show, but didn't find the energy to go to bed until 10 p.m.

I picked up my two new black kittens, Boris and Natasha, and carried them upstairs, one on each shoulder. Boris cried incessantly. He did not want to be shut up in the back wing of the house. Natasha was more compliant and nuzzled into my neck, purring. Jeff and I decided a long time ago that, to sleep undisturbed, we couldn't have two cats running around the house in the middle of the night or taking up space on our queen-sized bed. We needed to get a good night's sleep. They could race around the attic all night long, perform their sentry duties with a high view over the driveway and street, or they could curl up in old furniture and sleep in comfort.

I shut the door behind me and heard them scamper down the back hall and scurry up the attic stairs. I undressed, performed my nightly rituals, and climbed in to bed.

Just after 11 p.m., Jeff came to bed. He didn't purposely wake me but I heard him shuffling around the room. I stirred, letting him know that I could hear him.

"I just saw a mouse," he said in astonishment.

I opened an eye. "You did? Where?"

"It went behind my dresser." He grabbed a flashlight from his nightstand and pointed the beam behind the Spanish-style, solid oak highboy. He bent over but didn't want to put his face too close to the floor in case the mouse decided to jump out.

"See anything?" I asked.

"Where the hell did it go?" He paused. "Did you see it come out?" He was more than a little nervous about having this vermin in our room. Heck, he was obsessive about spiders biting him under the covers.

"No." I contemplated whether I really cared. I didn't. I turned over and said, "It's just a mouse. Come to bed." I fell back to sleep and didn't think another thing about it.

The alarm woke me at 5 a.m. *Strange. The cats let me sleep,"* I thought. In fact, even after I went to the bathroom, the cats were silent. They must have been really tired, I concluded. They were usually my automatic alarm, yowling and banging on the door just prior to 5 a.m.

I opened the door to the back hallway. Swoosh! The cats ran out and down the stairs at full speed!

I blinked in astonishment. Then I suddenly remembered. "The mouse!" I ran down the honey-colored staircase after them, ignoring my back, knee, and foot pain.

The cats cornered the mouse in the dining room by the swinging door to the kitchen. I groaned, imagining a chase through my precious collectibles or, worse, a chewed-up, bloody carcass on my Tabriz oriental carpet.

I had to see the mouse for myself. I debated whether to get a broom or other implement to smack it. Or perhaps

I should wake up Jeff and let him handle this. *"No,"* I thought, *"time is not on my side. I have to deal with this immediately."* I didn't want the mouse to dive under the radiator or slip under the door to the basement where it could hide for days.

Suddenly the mouse ran toward the front door. *"My goodness, this mouse is awfully big!"* I thought, after seeing its long tail race past my slipper.

It cowered in a tiny corner, the cats hissing but not attacking. I wondered if this was a rat! I really didn't know. I had never seen a rat. What I did know was that I didn't want it to bite my kittens! And I couldn't go to work with this thing loose in my house! I had to take action. Nothing else mattered.

With my left hand, I grabbed the mouse, er, rat by its tail. Somehow I knew it would curl up and bite me and I was right. Blood was starting to drip from several bites on my wrist and hand. So, I grabbed its long gray body with my right hand. It bit me a few times on the fingers. I was a total mess.

I opened the vestibule door and intended to throw it out the front door. I stopped in my tracks.

Damn! The alarm! I had forgotten that the security system was activated so I couldn't just open the front door. (In hindsight, I had several seconds before the alarm would go off, but it didn't occur to me.)

I switched hands holding the rat. It bit me several more times and now I was bleeding heavily from both hands. With bloody fingers, I punched in the code on the security panel. I opened the door and threw the rat as far as I could. When it landed, it scurried down the driveway and into the neighbor's bushes. (I could almost hear my neighbor Nicki saying, "Gee. Thanks, Ella," in a dry, sarcastic tone.)

When I was sure the rat was no longer a threat, I ran back in the house and screamed up the stairway, "Jefffff!" I held my hands away from my body so that my nightgown would not be ruined.

No response.

"Jeff," I screamed again. "Come down here! I'm bleeding!"

"What?" he asked groggily. "You're bleeding? From what?" I could hear his footfalls on the floor above.

"The rat bit me!"

"The rat? What rat? You mean the mouse?" He ran down the steps and stared aghast at my bloody hands.

"I think it was a rat!"

"You're kidding me."

"No."

"You'd better wash your hands good! How the hell did it bite you?" I told him the story as I headed for the kitchen. He couldn't believe that I would do such a stupid thing. But he wisely never said the words.

After washing my hands several times with anti-bacterial soap and treating the bites with Polysporin, I wrapped my hands in clean towels. "I'd better call the doctor." I looked at the clock. It was 5:30 a.m. I said to myself, *"The doctor is going to love hearing from me at this hour. Oh well, too bad."* My hands were shaking as I looked up and dialed the emergency phone number and got Dr. Gangemi's service.

It wasn't long before Dr. Gangemi returned the call. "I think a rat bit me," I explained.

"A rat?"

"Or a really big mouse."

"How the hell did that happen?" Obviously, no sympathy.

I told him a very abbreviated story. "You'd better come in to see me this morning. When was your last tetanus shot?" I told him it was on my 30th birthday. "Well, guess what? This is your lucky day." I hung up, showered, wrapped both hands in bandages, and dressed for work. The bites stung immensely.

Later, Jeff called me at work to see how I was doing. I admitted that I told a few close associates about my encounter, and how they all thought I was nuts.

"Ratfinger..." Jeff sang with a James Bond melody. Very funny. Not.

I told him I had appointment at 10 a.m. with Dr. Gangemi and that I'd call him back afterwards.

Seeing the doctor eye to eye was a bit embarrassing. Dr. Gangemi was a tall, good-looking, fit man in his late 50s. He had a way of staring right into your soul with his big, brown eyes. He washed his hands in the sink in the corner of the neutral-colored room and dried them with a paper towel. I sat on the examining table and extended my hands. He looked them over carefully, turning them front to back, and shook his head. I was betting that I was going to be the topic of conversation at his next doctor's seminar! It was one for the books.

"Do you think it really was a rat? Mice can get pretty big," he said very calmly. There was that stare again.

"This was the biggest damn mouse, then," I blurted, sure that I was not mistaken. "What about rabies?" Other diseases, like plague, went through my mind as well.

166

"You don't have to worry about rabies. A mouse or rat would not survive any length of time. You just have to worry about infection." After swabbing and re-bandaging my hands, he turned to a small metal table and prepared the tetanus shot.

The needle was quick. My arm was sore. I should have cowered in my office cubicle when I got back to work, but I was rather proud that I had been brave enough to grab a rat with my bare hands. I showed my wounds with pride.

Our Whiz Kid

ERIC'S FIRST WORD WAS NOT "Dada" or "Mama"; it was "radio." We knew right away that he would have a strong interest in electronics. Whenever we took a road trip, he always wanted to stop at all the Radio Shack stores along the way.

We got our first computer, a Radio Shack TRS-80, in 1979. Jeff and Eric played games on it, but Eric took it to a new level. He said, at age 10, that he could communicate with people around the world and even order airline tickets! I thought, *"No way."* But he showed me what he could do and I was very surprised and also very wary. He also learned Pascal and other computer languages on his own and began to write computer programs.

When we moved to Seneca Parkway, he became friends with Greg Winter, who had similar interests. They would walk to the "candy store" on the corner of Ave D and Conkey Avenue to buy electronics and soon his bedroom and our spacious attic were filled with motherboards, power supplies, microprocessors, etc. They set up their own company, Wintek Laser Laboratories, and also developed a laser and laser light show. At school, Eric won a Mobil Research award for his light-show entry and was asked to participate at the State Level. However, the boys needed a panel truck to transport all their equipment and the ONLY people the school permitted to drive the truck were his parents—as in me and Jeff. And unfortunately, Jeff was on a business trip. There was no way I could drive a stickshift truck to Albany, and so Eric's award went "up in smoke." I felt terrible about it and tried to convince the school principal to let Greg's father drive, but my request was denied since Greg attended a different school.

Greg went on to create and run the laser light show at High Falls in the city of Rochester.

Eric also won the Branda Frasier research competition for his technical writing abilities and it earned him a Monroe Community College class award.

After graduation in 1987, Eric worked for Optical Gauging Products, Harris Communications, The Stereo Shop, and SenDEC Corporation, which eventually separated and his company became Global Digital Instruments. GDI designs OEM electronic digital instrumentation for various vehicle industries. There, Eric invented a meter for measuring racecar performance and was featured in a *National Karting News* magazine article.

Eric became engaged to Hannelore Witt and were married June 22, 1996. The night before the wedding, they had a rehearsal at the Plantation Party House gazebo that went without a hitch.

After rehearsal, Marc Rumsey, Eric's Best Man, decided to go out for a few drinks. Unfortunately, he had a few too many. Leaving his car behind at the bar, he walked home. The next morning, the day of the wedding, Marc woke up, not feeling very well. He dressed in his tuxedo then went out to the driveway and discovered that his car wasn't there. It was slowly coming back to him that he left his car at the bar—if only he could remember which bar! He jumped on his bicycle, in his tux, and headed for downtown Rochester. He eventually found his car and drove to Eric's house to pick him up. They drove to the party house and, just as they pulled in, the car died. It ran out of gas!

The weather was a bigger issue. That morning a tornado touched down and there were multiple thunderstorms. Eric and Hanne were forced to have the wedding inside the restaurant instead of the gazebo. The lights flickered during the brief ceremony and I worried about a power outage and the chicken that was cooking in the ovens! Thankfully, the lights stayed on and everything else went according to plan.

Congratulations to Mr. & Mrs. Eric Stevens!

Jeff, Hanne, Eric, and Me

Movies

AROUND 1972, the hours-long movie *War and Peace* premiered on television for the first time. We gathered around the television at my parents' house to watch the classic film.

After three hours, Patty, who was around 12 or 13 years old, started to get frustrated. She said, "I've been watching this for three hours and I still haven't seen Warren Peace!"

Haha!

* * * * * *

In 1999 Marcia, Patty, and I decided to go to the Regal Cinema in Irondequoit to see *The Haunting* with Liam Neeson. It wasn't very good, yet quite memorable for us.

The theater was mostly empty, with perhaps 12 people besides us.

There was a scene when Liam's character, Dr. David Marrow, mentioned "Uncle Hugh Crain." Patty was confused and said aloud, "Uncle Ukraine?" Marcia and I started laughing and we couldn't stop. We had the giggles to the point where we couldn't breathe.

The people several rows back were upset that we were laughing (and I can understand that), and before I knew it, an empty soda bottle hit me in the head then rolled down the aisle. That made me laugh even harder.

When the movie was over, we walked out of the "horror show" laughing so hard, tears were rolling down our cheeks. The people going into the theater probably wondered if they were going in to see the right movie. LOL

Life on
Bald Eagle Drive

Kendall, NY
1999-Present

Dream of a Lake House

ON A SUNDAY MORNING IN JUNE 1999, when we were living on Seneca Parkway, Jeff and I were browsing the multiple listings page on the internet, as we did often. I found one listing particularly intriguing. Not the house itself, but the illusion it gave. It was as if the house weren't there at all. Sure, there were walls, but that's not what you saw. When you looked through the front windows and out the back, all you saw was the lake—Lake Ontario.

The house was an "L"-shaped 50s ranch (and I truly detested ranch houses) sitting on one acre. The house was barely 1,500 square feet. No basement, no real attic. There was a pole barn on the other side of the road, but what was a pole barn anyway? We put the listing aside.

Yet, it kept calling to me.

I remembered the picnic for Aunt Jean's 80th birthday the summer before. Patty had just gone to a psychic, Jeani Wesp, and she wanted me to hear her tape.

"You've got to hear part of my tape," Patty beckoned. "I brought it with me."

I wasn't quite convinced that it was necessary. "Why? What did she say?"

"She says you're moving!"

175

Now she piqued my interest! "You're kidding! Let's go hear it!"

We slipped away from the party being held in my cousin Gayle's back yard. Patty's van was parked on the street. I climbed into the passenger side while Patty sat behind the wheel. She turned the key so that the tape player would work on the car's battery.

(Patty) "What can you tell me about my sister?"

(Jeani) "What is her name?"

(Patty) "Eloise Stevens."

(Jeani) "She's going to move, west. Toward Hilton, Hamlin—I see an H."

At the time, I was quite shocked at this revelation since we hadn't been serious about house hunting. It was quite true that we had driven along the Lake Ontario State Parkway because we thought of living on the lake, but nothing ever came of it.

So now, here was a house on the lake. The private street was at the end of Norway Road in Orleans County. I groaned at the thought of driving into work from the next county.

"Do you want to try to find Bald Eagle Drive?" I asked. Jeff wasn't ready to drive that far, though.

Jeff replied, "Maybe we should get Jim G. to start looking for us." Jim was our real estate agent when we bought the house on Seneca Parkway. A few days later, Jim gave us a listing of several houses to check out but it didn't include the house on Bald Eagle.

Since I was really into birds, I liked the street name. It also was a fine Indian totem, one of two that were in psychic readings for me. My other totem was the Horse. One of the psychics I went to, Bernice Golden, said that I'd be surrounded by horses some day.

In response to her vision, I said, "But I don't even like horses."

She said, "I know. But you will live in a place where there are horses all around you. They give you strength."

The next weekend I again asked Jeff, "Do you want to check out that house on Bald Eagle Drive?" They had an open house. He agreed to drive out there.

The June day was bright and sunny, with a mild breeze, a perfect day for a drive. We passed Hamlin Beach State Park and I thought of Patty's tape. We got off the Parkway at the next exit, Morton, on Route 272 or County Line Road. I had never heard of Morton, but my mother had a cousin named Helen Morton. I wondered if the town was named after a relative.

We passed by a small corral with two horses in it; I thought of the psychic's prediction. It wasn't that close to the house, though, so I could hardly be "surrounded by horses." When we got to the lake, we made a left and drove down the one-lane country road until we saw the For Sale sign. We were shocked to find out that the realtor worked in the same office as ours—Caldwell Banker, Royal Oak! It was even more perplexing why Jim didn't give us this listing.

My first impression of the house took my breath away! The panoramic view of the lake was dramatic with nothing to block your vision. All the windows were open and the breeze was gently blowing the gauzy white curtains, which were entwined with pink and blue ribbons, floating in the breeze. There was a back door directly across from the entry to lead you to the lake. The lady realtor was sitting at a glass dinette table wearing a flowing white dress that also gently blew in the breeze. The dreaminess was all part of the "package."

Bald Eagle Drive, Kendall, NY

A new turquoise carpet covered the open living space and met a bleached driftwood vinyl floor in the kitchen and hallway areas. The paneled walls were painted white and the kitchen cabinets were a white European-style with gray barnwood trim (ugh). The house was decorated in a modern Southwest style with lots of glass accents and a gray leather sectional sofa. I was immediately attracted to a mirror in the dining space that was Asian in design. It matched my entertainment center!

The master bedroom was small, but I noted that the owner had all the furniture pieces we did—a queen-size bed, a highboy, a triple dresser, and two nightstands—so I knew our furniture would fit. There was also a nice walk-in closet. The main bathroom was across the hall and very compact— no tub, just a shower enclosure. I didn't care for the wallpaper but I could deal with that temporarily.

The second bedroom needed a lot of work, but it had a good-sized closet. There was an itsy-bitsy powder room across the hall that could barely fit one person. The toilet tank was cracked and I could see that blue toilet cleaner was leaking through. The third advertised bedroom wasn't a bedroom at all. It was being used as a mud/laundry/mechanical room and office. It was very ugly, but that could be fixed.

One closet contained the well pump. We were told public water had been installed a few years earlier, but the well could still be used outside for washing cars or watering the lawn. The house had a septic system.

We walked out the side door to wander around the property. We headed straight for the lake, of course. The frontage was about 90 feet deep and wide, with a steep slope to a rocky shore.

"Oh my God, how do they mow that?" I said. It looked very dangerous. One slip and you'd be bouncing off the huge Medina-stone boulders. We were told that the boulders were put in place after Hurricane Agnes to prevent further erosion. Apparently, a boathouse had been there at one time—the footings were still evident. I was disappointed that there was no easy way to get to the water without climbing down the rocks, and there was no "beach" to speak of, just rocks.

The pole barn was huge. It looked like they had used it for parties rather than a place to house their vehicles.

In the back of the garage, was a stretch of grass and trees and I imagined bluebirds fluttering around and a great garden with a wandering path. I loved the wide-open space!

They get you when you start to dream. And dream I did.

We didn't make an offer right away though, as we had to put our house on the market and try to sell it. It was August 15 before we actually put in an offer and it was accepted, with the contingency that we sell our house first. We went out two more times just to look around.

Trying to keep our house on Seneca ready for showing was challenging and I was exhausted from constantly cleaning and shuffling the cats to the attic. Plus, I was packing and my back and knees were killing me. I actually showed the house to a female police officer, and I was hoping she'd be interested, but no offer came.

In late September, Jim called us to say that another realtor wanted to present us with an offer at the house with her client. I was uncomfortable about this arrangement because you don't have the freedom of private discussions. They sat around our dining room table and the client was a young, single woman ("P"), which surprised me.

They low-balled us by about $30,000. Without even looking at Jeff, I got up and said, "Let me show you to the door." Shock registered on all their faces and I heard Jim say, "No, no! Let's talk about this." They tried to tell us that we lived in a crime-ridden area, etc. I wasn't falling for it. We did come down in price $15,000 and signed the deal, but we felt "taken."

Packing started in earnest. Closing was set for early November. Our lawyer called us to say that we had never obtained a permit for our gazebo and we couldn't close without it. So, I had to go to City Hall and apply for a permit. They said they needed a "stick" description before they would approve it. In a panic, I went back to my office on State St, looked up the Rick's gazebo place in Pennsylvania on the internet, called them, and asked them to fax over the stick description. They did so immediately and I had to go back to City Hall to get the approval, which I did.

Another call from the lawyer came the next day. We couldn't close when we wanted because "P", the owner-to-be, had not paid her federal income taxes on the 13 properties she owned. I was furious! However, it did buy us more time to pack. We also made an arrangement to move into Bald Eagle Drive and pay rent until the actual closing.

I had cleaned out and packed up the attic the day before, without throwing out much. We still hadn't started the basement or the garage! When the movers showed up on Saturday, Jeff just had them pack up everything from the garage. The movers almost killed themselves moving Jeff's toolbox up the basement stairs.

I went ahead to the house on Bald Eagle Drive to await the moving van. I remember unlocking the door and walking into the empty space and feeling joy. I had no place to sit except the window seat. My new next-door neighbor Betsy, from my Kodak department, came over with cookies. I was very appreciative since we hadn't had anything to eat all day.

I was most concerned with my dining room table and told the movers it was my pride and joy and it didn't have a scratch on it. The (new) guy who was packing the van took charge of the table and broke two of its legs. I sat down and cried. The other mover felt bad for me and allowed me to fill out an insurance form after the fact so that I could get the table repaired. (The repair didn't work.)

In the end, they filled the moving van and still had a ton of stuff sitting in our old house that we had to move ourselves.

I was still cleaning the house when "P" called, asking if she could put a few things in our dining room. I told her our insurance didn't cover her things, but she said she didn't care. I asked Jeff and he wasn't happy about it, but we agreed to let her put a few things in the dining room. We were shocked to find her pulling into our driveway with a moving van! She started taking things up to the attic, etc. It wasn't what we agreed to! I was furious. I told her I was still cleaning, and she told me, "Oh don't bother."

Jeff and I took several trips until we were satisfied that we had everything. Eric helped us with the last trip, agreeing to transport the two cats in a cage and me. Wouldn't you know it, the cats did not travel well and ended up having bowel movements. It reeked for 30 miles! Gag!

The next day I called my lawyer about "P"'s belongings. He said she needed to pay rent. She disconnected her phone and wouldn't pick up on her cell phone when he tried to reach her, so she got away without paying anything!

We finally closed on November 18, and "P" called me afterward to say that she found a few things of mine—a linen closet full of stuff and negatives wrapped in aluminum foil in the fridge. (My wedding pictures!) We went back to pick them up and she showed us around the house. Not my taste, for sure, but it was her house now.

A week after we moved in, I noticed a big hole outside the bathroom window. The septic tank cover had fallen in! We discovered that the tank was actually a rusty, perforated, old oil tank that didn't meet code. We had to replace our entire septic system. Just swell.

Well, I had my serene Lake house to go home to every night. As soon as I saw the blue water on the horizon in my drive home from work, I calmed down and let go of all my stress. It was wonderful. And soon I put in that garden in back of the barn. It was my "secret garden," a retreat for my spirit, and a place of serenity.

My Secret Garden

Living on the lake, however, was "heaven" and "hell." Heaven, obviously, to be on a permanent vacation at the lake. Hell during the winter. Our house acted like a snow fence. You might see green grass on the lawn, but not be able to exit the house. The snow accumulated around the house, blocking all our exits. There were times I had to climb out the kitchen window (which was only about 18 inches off the ground). Jeff would hand me the shovel and I would shovel my way around the house to the driveway door. Once the snowdrift against the door was cleared, I could then open the door and have an exit in case of emergency. Most people can exit through their garage, but our "garage" was across the road!

One February morning I walked into the living room and looked at the kitchen window. There was no way Jeff could go to work—the snow was up to the top of the window! There were other times when I'd shovel out, just to get snowed in again. I learned to get up every two hours at night to shovel out the driveway door during storms like that.

Once, again in February, I shoveled for nine hours until I screamed to the heavens above to "STOP!" It did! Somebody was listening!

All in all, living on Bald Eagle Drive has been a wonderful experience. Who knows what the future will bring? But for now, this is home.

Me with Natasha and Boris

September 11, 2001

I WOULD BE REMISS IF I didn't mention 9/11. People ask, "Where were you when you heard about the attack?" Everyone has a story.

It was a glorious late summer day, blue skies and shining sun. I went to work at Kodak, as usual. Just after 8:46 a.m., Sue M., a co-worker, came running to my office saying, "Terrorists have attacked the Twin Towers in New York! A plane crashed into the building and it's on fire!"

I quickly went to the internet and saw the whole thing unfold: The planes crashing, the people covered in soot exiting the towers, the firefighters, police, and EMTs trying to do their jobs and dying for it. The horror of it! It was terrifying. Everyone was glued to the ongoing situation. You could only imagine what was happening to the thousands of people in those buildings. We all prayed silently for them. Then there was the plane headed for Washington, D.C. (perhaps the Capital Building), which was stopped by the passengers. The cry was, "Let's roll!" spoken by Todd Beamer, a passenger onboard Flight 93. They were successful in stopping the terrorists on that flight, but everyone ended up dying in a field in Pennsylvania. The Pentagon was also struck, causing a massive fire.

President George Bush was reading to little children in a class in Florida when he was informed of the attack. He didn't want to alarm the children, so he finished the story and then met with his advisors.

People in my office were overwhelmed with sadness. Many could no longer work and went home. I wasn't allowed to go home, as I had a meeting with a difficult client at MEC on East River Road, along with my team. She refused to cancel the meeting. After the meeting, I almost had a car crash as someone laid on their horn and I didn't know if they were directing it at me. I overreacted and almost hit a pickup truck!

When I got home, I was shaking from both the day's events, the near accident, and the dread that comes with the unknown. I didn't sleep a wink that night. I was reading a Stephen King book about terrorists in NYC and decided not to finish it. Starting that day, I could no longer watch the national news. I found it too depressing.

Going Up the Ladder

AS I MENTIONED EARLIER IN this book, I started at Kodak as a secretary in 1966. In June 1968 I left to get married, but returned to Kodak in 1971 to work in Market Research & Analysis. In the early 80s, the need for secretaries was dwindling, so I was assigned as an Administrative Assistant, running IBM reports, communicating with our sales force, and handling requests from Litigation. In 1984 I transferred from Market Research to Publications, working for Paul Mulroney. Within a couple of years, I was handling Commercial Photography book sales with our Distributors in the U.S. and traveled with Paul and Keith Boas to St. Louis where we did an inventory check and met with the team there.

Publications went through several management changes, but I had supervisors who worked to promote me. For a few years I was a proofreader for all the photography books, technical publications, and newsletters that went through the department. I loved that job and it gave me insight and experience on the process for bringing a publication to press, including checking press sheets through local printers.

In the 1990s, I worked closely with Suzanne Blessing, our graphic artist, and Joseph Janowicz, a marketing editor, on several jobs, including the Professional Photography Division newsletter, *PPD Today*. Whenever we completed a project, we'd celebrate by going to a famous Rochester "institution" for lunch—Nick Tahou's—a hot dog and burger restaurant downtown, noted for its "Garbage Plate"—two hots (red or white) or burgers, and any combination of macaroni salad, baked beans, or french fries. Nick Tahou began to recognize me and Joseph, and one day, Nick saw us and exclaimed, "The beauty and the beast!" LOL. On another occasion, Nick sat with a group of us and Joseph took a picture of me and Nick that I still treasure today.

Me and Nick Tahou

Another time, a TV food show, *Unwrapped*, was shooting at Nick Tahou's and I went there with co-workers Jean

Wallace and Renee Nobles and Renee's sister Jane to check it out. Jean's comment on the Garbage Plate made the cut for their "Funny Foods" segment and it was on TV!

After a couple of years, there was another reorganization and our department ended up in a new division. It was at that time that my supervisor, Sue Lees, along with management, promoted me to Technical Editor. I worked on Motion Picture publications, slide projector technical information, newsletters, and later Kodak Professional digital cameras. After another reorganization, I became a project manager (with Derek Doeffinger as my supervisor) and worked with a team that sent out daily e-mails to any consumer who bought and registered a Kodak digital camera. I loved this job, too, but it was extremely demanding. After three years as project manager, and 33 years with Kodak, I decided to retire.

It was time to cut the cord, but I kept in touch with many of the girls like Suzanne, Jean, Renee, Mary-Helen Maginn Finn, and Judy Caysinger.

Starry, Starry Night

IT WAS 4:30 A.M. WHEN OUR phone rang.

I was quite groggy and stiff, but I made my way around the bed toward the phone. Jeff picked it up before I got to it.

He said into the receiver, "So you're at the hospital now? Uh-huh. Okay. Here. Your mother wants to talk to you." He handed me the phone.

"Hi," I said rather hoarsely, trying to clear my throat.

Eric said, "Well, I just wanted you to know we're at the hospital."

"Is Hanne in hard labor?" I asked.

"No, no, not at all."

"How much is she dilated?"

"One!" he laughed.

"I guess it'll be a while yet."

I told him we'd see him later, anticipating that he'd let us know when the baby arrived.

I turned off the alarm, fed the cats, and got into the shower. Today was the day. Tuesday, August 12, 2003. I thought, *"Twelve. That's a good even number and when added together it's three, my lucky number."*

We had been on pins and needles waiting for this call. A week earlier, as we vacationed in Cape May, New Jersey, I prayed that the baby would not arrive early. It was important for me to go to Cape May, not just for relaxation, but to meet up with Jerry M.—my pen pal whom I had not seen in 30 years. The fifteen minutes we had chatting and hugging was worth the trip.

Now this was truly a magical day. I got dressed for work and looked at the calendar on the refrigerator. A full moon! No surprise. Eric was born on a full moon, too. However, today, not only was there a full moon, but a sky sprinkled with shooting stars from the comet Swift-Tuttle, and Mars outshining everything in the night sky. In the early morning, the moon and Mars slid high into the southern sky, then toward dawn, they drifted lower and to the southwest, with Mars well above and to the left of the moon. The moon set as day broke, while Mars stayed above the horizon and gradually paled. The Perseid meteor shower was due to peak overnight Tuesday into Wednesday morning.

At 6 a.m. it was already hot. The day was going to be a scorcher. I drove into work and told Renee Nobles and others what the situation was, although I fully intended to work the whole day. I was amazingly relaxed.

About 9:30 a.m. I ended one meeting and was preparing for a nasty 11 o'clock meeting with a client when the phone rang. It was Christa, Hanne's mom.

"Hanne's starting hard labor," she said. "I think you ought to get over to the hospital."

"Okay. Have you called Jeff?"

"I tried calling him at home, but the line is busy."

"I'll get ahold of him," I promised.

I shot off a quick note to my co-workers saying, "The baby is on its way!" and made a hasty departure, grabbing my bag in case I wouldn't be coming back (even though I told them I would).

Every few seconds, I tried Jeff on our home phone, since he was unemployed at the time. Still busy. He was probably trying to get some work. When I got to the car, I called his cell. It was off. I headed down Lake Avenue facing construction all the way to Driving Park and a single lane of traffic. Luckily, I had the air conditioning on full blast to keep cool and I made good time. I pulled into Rochester General Hospital's parking garage and tried Jeff again. This time I got through.

"Hanne's delivering!"

"Oh, yeah?"

"Christa called me at work. Hanne's starting hard labor."

"Where are you? Should I pick you up?"

"No. I'm in the hospital parking garage already. Just come down."

"Okay. See ya."

I walked as fast as my legs would take me. I went up to the Information Desk, and asked for Hanne's room. Very turtle-like, the receptionist slowly looked her up on the computer. I thought I would never get it, but finally she smiled and said, "She's in her room and that can only mean one thing!" She handed me a slip with the room number. *"Oh no,"* I thought. *"She must have had the baby already!"* I raced down the hallways, zig-zagging around people, following the yellow ceiling tabs for the yellow elevator. Of course, both yellow elevators were already going up and

I had to wait endlessly, it seemed, for the next one. I impatiently poked the elevator button several times.

I was cognizant of a tall man standing behind me in a brown suit, and he was apparently waiting for the elevator along with several others. When I got on the elevator, I heard a gentle, "Hello!" I looked up and there was my former GP, Dr. Gangemi! I had briefly scanned his nametag and then felt embarrassed that I even looked. I'm sure he was aware of my uncertainty. "Oh my God! Dr. Gangemi! How are you?" I gave him a hug and then covered up my emotional greeting with my excuse: "I'm about to be a grandmother! My son's wife is delivering as we speak!"

"Well, congratulations!" he said with sincerity.

We exchanged pleasantries on how nice it was to see each other, then I dashed off the elevator. I suddenly thought, *"Did I just hug my doctor?"*

Christa was waiting outside the room. "She's in a lot of pain."

"So, she hasn't delivered yet?" I glanced at the sign outside of Hanne's room, announcing "Stork at work!"

"Not yet," Christa replied.

I walked in the large room with two big windows to find three hospital workers diligently performing their duties and telling Hanne how to breathe. Eric was beside her, holding her hand. He was doing remarkably well (no fainting, no dizziness, no stress). Hanne acknowledged me then was sidetracked by another painful contraction.

Puzzled, I looked at Christa. "Are they delivering the baby right here in her room?"

"Yep. That's what they do these days."

Over the next fifteen minutes, we watched Hanne as she went through a few more contractions. I was wringing my hands in sympathy, remembering well how I felt during Eric's birth.

I asked Christa if Emil, Hanne's dad, was coming. She said that Emil was supposed to take care of Hans' (Hanne's brother) kids, but Margaret (Hans' wife) had to make other arrangements for them so he could come to the hospital. Emil would be along shortly. I figured it would take Jeff 45 minutes, so I wasn't expecting him too soon.

All of a sudden, we heard this awful noise! A jackhammer! Every so often, construction workers on the floor below would start drilling. *DRRRRRRRT! DRRRRRRRT!* It was terribly disconcerting. What a way to come into this world, hearing that god-awful sound!

After five minutes or so, the doctor in charge started giving orders. He requested the pediatrician. He gave Hanne a local anesthetic and told her to start pushing. Eric's arm was getting cramped and numb, trying to support her leg. Christa and I had to get out of the way to make room for several other workers who suddenly appeared, so we slipped behind a rocker where we could watch the delivery. *DRRRRRRRT!* The jackhammering continued.

The obstetrician determined that the baby needed help and requested suction. Within seconds and with another push, we saw the obstetrician pull the baby out and up. Although we could barely hear with all the jackhammering, Eric turned to us and said proudly, "It's a girl!"

Christa and I exclaimed, "It's a girl!" and we hugged. The time was 10:46 a.m. The workers made fast work of cutting the cord, suctioning out mucus from the baby's air passages, and treating her eyes. After cleaning her up and wrapping her in pink, blue and white swaddling clothes, they handed her to Hanne. I immediately thought of Eric's birth, when the nurse handed Eric to Jeff first and the jealousy I felt (and never got over, obviously). Eric started taking pictures of the new mom and the baby.

Eric and Hanne knew they wanted to name the baby Amanda, but were still unsure of her middle name. They had a list of pretty names, but quickly ruled out Sarah (initials would be ASS). Of all the names, Danielle rolled off the tongue better than the others. They didn't want to choose a name of a relative, but I reminded them that Danielle was Shannon's middle name. "Oh well," resigned Eric. "It's just a middle name." I thought Shannon would be pleased to hear they chose Danielle.

Shortly after the delivery, Emil arrived, then Jeff. The baby was handed to Eric and then to each of the proud grandparents. We have pictures to savor those moments. When I held Amanda, she seemed to be looking right at me, her eyes scanning me from right to left. I thought, "Binary baby!" Eric snapped a picture with his digital camera. He must have shot at least 100 pictures that day.

I said, "You kids did good work. She's perfect!" And she was. No squished, red face. Amanda had big, beautiful blue eyes and creamy white skin. Reddish hair peeked out from her knitted bonnet and her ruby red lips looked like she was wearing lipstick. She was 19 inches long (a little peanut) and weighed 6 lbs. 10 oz., just like Eric.

It wasn't long before the nurse wanted Hanne to begin breastfeeding, so we were all ushered out of the room. It gave us the chance to use the restroom and pick up lunch in the cafeteria. We spent a little more time with Hanne and Amanda before saying goodbye and letting them rest.

Feeling the pride and joy, I decided to stop by Marcia's place of employment, The Shire at Culverton. I parked my car near the entrance, walked in, and told the girl at the desk that I was there to see Marcia Fedyk and that I was her sister. She pointed me to the office area on the left where some women were eating their lunch. Marcia was in her office so they opened the door and said, "Your sister is here."

Marcia said, "No...My sister?" She looked perplexed when she walked out of her office. "Why are you here?" she asked.

"I'm a grandma!" I announced.

"You're a grandma? Oh boy! I wondered when the baby was due."

"A little girl—Amanda Danielle."

"A little girl? How cute! When?"

"About 10:45 this morning." It was now about 1 o'clock.

"Have you gone to the hospital?"

"I just came from there and now I'm headed back to work." I gave Marcia the room number so that she could visit Hanne if she had time.

After introductions to the staff and a few baby details, I said my goodbyes and headed back to work.

Everyone at work was surprised to see me back. Of course, I was so pumped up that I didn't work very much that afternoon. I made phone calls to Patty, Mickey, and my girlfriend Jeanne, and I downloaded some pictures and printed them out on laser paper (I didn't have any photo paper with me). I hung my favorite picture on my cubicle wall for the world to see! My boss Derek thought Amanda looked just like me! I left early to get my hair done (a scheduled appointment) and to race home so that Jeff and I could drive to the hospital together.

When we arrived at the hospital, Eric's friend Marc Rumsey and Hanne's parents showed up at the same time. Hanne was breastfeeding so we headed down to the cafeteria again, where we bought Eric and Marc dinner.

"Eric, did you go home and take a nap?" I asked.

"Well, I had to go home to let the dog out, but I didn't sleep."

"I saw Marcia and told her about the baby."

"Yeah. Hanne said she came to see the baby this afternoon. We wondered how she found out so quickly."

Christa and I compared notes on delivering our kids, a favorite subject for most women, and we had a few laughs, much to Eric's embarrassment.

Up in the hospital room, we held Amanda again and marveled at her beauty.

Eric was looking at me strangely. "Am I mistaken, or is your hair a different color tonight?"

I laughed. "You're not nuts. I had a hair appointment this afternoon and had my hair dyed!"

"Geez, the baby saw you blonde this afternoon, and red tonight. You're confusing her!"

We left when the 8 p.m. bell rang, but Eric and Marc stayed on. Later, the night nurse told Marc he'd have to leave. Eric decided to go home, too, and get some sleep. As he and Marc reached the parking garage, Eric discovered he left his wallet at home and Marc had no money! And Eric had purposely left his cell phone home since they were prohibited in the hospital.

They debated what to do. Eric knew he could go back up to the room and get money from Hanne's purse, but Marc couldn't go with him. When Eric tried to go back into the hospital, the doors were locked.

"Maybe they take Visa," Marc said. So, they got in their cars and headed for the attendant.

"Do you take Visa?" Marc asked.

"No. Just cash."

"We can't get back in the hospital to get to my friend's wife's room. Er, can we pay you tomorrow?"

"No. Sorry."

Eric and Marc re-parked their cars and discussed their next step. They didn't even have a quarter for a phone call. And who would they call? Were they doomed to stay in the parking garage all night?

Finally, they got the bright idea to walk around the hospital to the emergency room so Eric could get back to Hanne's room. As they walked into the emergency room, Marc noticed a Krispy Kreme vending machine and was thinking, *"Yum. I wish I had money for a doughnut."*

They both stopped in their tracks. Above the vending machine was a lighted red sign that said "ATM." They couldn't believe their eyes.

Disgusted, Eric asked, "Now why couldn't the parking garage guy tell us there was an ATM here!"

Marc used his ATM card to get $20. When they got back to the parking garage, they discovered that the attendant was gone and the gates were up!

"He couldn't have told us that the gates would be open in a few minutes?" Marc groaned in disbelief.

They jumped in their cars and went home, barely noticing the light show in the night sky.

The Perseid meteor showers sprinkled the sky, the full moon shone brightly, and Mars beamed. What a miraculous day and night!

The day Eric brought Hanne and Amanda home from the hospital, we had a scorching heat wave, which caused a blackout on the east coast! I was in physical therapy for my knees when the power went out. I didn't need electricity so I continued with my exercises, working up a real sweat without air conditioning!

On the way home, I took the back roads to avoid tie-ups at intersections where the lights were out. I desperately needed gas, but all the gas stations were closed because they couldn't operate the pumps. Just past Hilton, I saw that the little station across from Dakota's Restaurant was open, and a stream of thirty cars or so were lined up on Route 18. I got in line. There were lots of people trying to buy ice or submarine sandwiches because they couldn't cook. Or they were filling up their boats or extra cans of gas for their farm or lawn equipment. It was probably a half hour when I pulled out, irritated with the people who were blocking the exit.

When I drove through Hamlin, I was very surprised to see that all the gas stations were operating, and busy. Hamlin had electricity! I debated whether to stop at the Chinese takeout, but decided against it.

I didn't have my hopes up for power in Kendall. My street was hooked up to an ancient and fragile grid and we lost power on a regular basis. However, when I got home, the garage door opened—we had power! I couldn't believe it.

Jeff was playing golf and probably had no idea that there was a blackout. And there were no delays in today's second round of the PGA championship at Oak Hill Country Club in Pittsford. Shaun Micheel went on to win the championship later that week.

I called Eric and found that they, unfortunately, did not have electricity.

"If the power doesn't come back on by 9 o'clock, I don't know how we're going to sleep," he grumbled.

"You could come out here," I offered.

"No, no. We just need to keep the baby comfortable. It's a good thing it's not winter."

Luckily, power was restored that evening, much to the relief of everyone on the east coast. The news programs had to broadcast using generators or inside trailers. The normally svelte newscasters were disheveled and sweaty. Everything was tacky. It was pathetic, but what else could they do? They showed millions of New Yorkers walking home across the bridges, reminiscent of 9/11, and other New Yorkers partying and drinking lots of iced-down beer.

Everyone's first thought of the blackout was "Terrorists!" but it proved to be a malfunction out of Cleveland, Ohio.

What a week it had been! Cape May, Jerry, the blackout, the PGA, the starry, starry nights, and above all else, little Amanda, my darling granddaughter. I finally got the little girl I prayed for all my life. I felt so blessed.

Good Times with Grandma

WHEN I RETIRED IN 2004, Eric and Hanne asked me to babysit on Mondays for little Amanda, who wasn't quite a year old. She wanted to be held a lot and cried when put in her crib. I used to lie on her bedroom floor and pretend I was going to sleep, and then she'd fall asleep.

We'd watch Baby Einstein/Baby Beethoven on TV and she loved it. I played a CD of nursery rhymes and sung them to her as we rocked in the rocking chair. She "rode" my leg as I bounced her up and down and sang *"Pony boy, Pony boy. Won't you be my pony* boy? Don't say no. Here we go, riding cross the plains. Marry me. Carry me. Right away with you! Giddy-up, giddy-up, giddy-up. Whoa! My pony boy!"*

*Original lyrics by Bobby Heath used the word *"Tony" boy.*

When Amanda was one year old, I sent a sweet picture of her to the Post Office to have a stamp made and put it on all of my Christmas cards. Hanne got the card but didn't notice the stamp, but Amanda did. "Manda!" she said. Hanne replied, "Yes, it's for Amanda." Amanda pointed to the envelope and said louder, "Manda!" Again, Hanne didn't know what she was talking about. Amanda yelled again, "Manda!" This time Hanne looked at the envelope and saw the stamp. She was very surprised but even more surprised that Amanda saw it right away.

If Amanda heard the garbage men, she'd wake up from her nap and insist on looking at them through the front window and waving to them. Sometimes one trash guy would wave back and she'd get excited. When she learned how to walk holding on to things, she'd run around her playpen, escaping my grasp, and laugh hysterically at her own cleverness. When she'd babble on her fake telephone, she'd push her imaginary "long" hair away from her face with her hand, just like her mom did. One of her favorite pastimes was playing with toys in the kitchen sink full of water. She'd splash around for an hour while I stood next to her, making sure she didn't fall off the kitchen chair. I'd also push her around in a kiddie "ice cream truck" in her kitchen. We played hide 'n seek and she'd always hide in the same place, except once she surprised me and hid in the clothes hamper! Amanda always wanted to wear my wedding ring, but I was afraid she'd put it down the heat register and it would be difficult to retrieve, so I stopped wearing it.

But Amanda and I had the most fun throwing soft cotton baby blocks at each other in the living room, like a snowball fight. We played that every time we were together.

She was definitely a little girl, loving pretty, sparkly things and very particular about her wardrobe. She even had her own pair of Crocs. When I bought imitation Crocs for myself, she closely examined them for the Crocs logo and, when she didn't see it, she yelled out, "Hey! These aren't 'Crocs'!! Take 'em back!" Haha.

Her mom had stored away the soft blocks so we looked for a replacement to use in our "snowball" fight. Amanda decided to try using her Crocs. After we had thrown them back and forth a few times, I was laughing while she threw one of the Crocs and it landed right in my open mouth! Perfect shot! I let it sit there as we both rolled over in laughter. Too bad she didn't have a camera!

When she was about 2 years old, I took her to L.A. Weight Loss with me. She put down her little pink purse (that matched her little pink outfit), jumped into the lap of the counselor, and started to tell her all about herself. When we got up to leave, she left her purse behind. The counselor said, "You forgot your purse!" Holding her hand to her mouth, Amanda gasped, "Oh no!" and went back into the room to grab it. So darn cute.

On her second Christmas, Jeff and I surprised her with her own kitchen set and fake food. Jeff and Eric put it together in the basement. Then Hanne and I distracted her in the living room, as the guys brought it up into the kitchen area. She walked into the kitchen and was absolutely stunned! One of her best gifts ever, even though she had to stretch to reach the "microwave." We played with it every week for years and she developed a strong interest in cooking and baking. (That's one thing I never developed no matter how much I played with the kitchen.)

I often read books to her and the first word she could identify was "Achoo!" As I was reading a Christmas book to her, I pointed to the word "Christmas" and asked her if she knew what word it was. I gave her a clue—it was said a lot during that time of year. Her answer? "Dot com." Haha. My son's daughter, for sure.

Eric, Hanne, 2-year-old Amanda, Jeff and I went to Chinatown restaurant for dinner one Saturday night.

Amanda expected the food to be put on the table immediately. When it wasn't, she saw the waiter in the aisle and yelled to him in her loudest voice, "Hey, Man! Hungry!!" She wasn't shy at all!

One day, when she was shy about putting on her tap shoes, I showed her how to tap dance by using my own made-up steps. She was horrified and had to show me how to do the proper steps using her tap shoes! Mission accomplished!

One of her favorite TV shows was *The Wiggles,* so Hanne, Amanda, and I went to see them live at the Blue Cross Arena in Rochester on August 29, 2005 (the same day that Hurricane Katrina struck New Orleans). When she saw them running around on stage and up and down the audience aisles, she was quite puzzled, not realizing that they were actual people. (Their concert was very funny and in my Top 3 favorite concerts!) Strangely, after the show, Amanda didn't want to watch them on TV again. They must have spooked her.

As she grew a little older, she loved dressing up. She found a purple negligee top (with spaghetti straps) in Hanne's drawer and figured it would make the loveliest princess gown! And it did. Hanne, Patty, and I bought her dress-up gowns: a pink and white ballerina dress, a wedding gown and veil, a "Belle" gown from Beauty and the Beast, a Little Mermaid gown, Tinkerbell costume, etc. Amanda and I played Little Mermaid for hours and hours and hours.

Amanda Playing Dress-Up

She was always Ariel, and I was always Prince Eric, King Triton, and the evil Ursula. We sometimes played Peter Pan. She was always Wendy, and I was always Peter, Wendy's brothers, Captain Hook, and all the other pirates. Once, we played Peter Pan in her front yard and she wanted me, as a pirate, to tie her to a tree. I just imagined the neighbors calling the police on me and told her that was out of the question. When we played inside, though, I loosely tied her up to a chair. (Don't call 911 on me!) When she dressed up in her wedding dress, I was always the groom. She had to walk down the aisle dozens of times, as I sang the tune "Here Comes the Bride" over and over.

Jeff, Hanne, and I took Amanda to Midtown Plaza at Christmas 2007 to let her ride Rochester's famous Monorail, just before they tore down the building.

I also took Amanda to the Seneca Park Zoo a few times where we sang my dad's song to the elephants: *"Oh, happy hours we have spent, looking at the elephants! Moo, moo, moo, moo. Moo, moo, moo."* She enjoyed wading in the little creek at the zoo, too. We also went to Museum of Science and Natural History, the Planetarium, and the Strong Museum. She loved the Wegmans grocery store at the Strong Museum, and when I asked her what she liked best about the museum, she said the girl at the Wegmans store, who was handicapped and in a wheelchair! She had a soft heart ♥.

Following in the footsteps of my dad, I wanted to show Amanda some places she had never seen before. We went to my friend Patty Becherer's place on Honeoye Lake, Grimes Glen in Naples, NY, to the Hemlock Lake Park (the most stunning, scenic view ever!), Hamlin Beach, Charlotte Beach, and Durand-Eastman Beach on Lake Ontario, Highland Park, Corning Museum of Glass, Brown's Berry Farm in Point Breeze, NY, the Lockport NY Caves, Ridge Road Station in Murray, NY, Erie Canal rides out of Corn Hill (the *Mary*

Jemison) and Lockport (the *Lockview*), the paddleboat ride on the *Harbor Belle* down the Genesee River, the Caledonia Fish Hatcheries, Lollipop Farm, a lighthouse in Sodus NY and a nearby farm animal rescue, the Hidden Valley Animal Adventure in Varysburg, NY, the Rundel Library in Rochester, the Herkimer Diamond Mines, and the Padre Pio church in Gates where she first saw Jesus hanging on the cross. I also treated her to a spa where she had her nails done, a sidewalk lunch on Park Avenue, lunch at a tea room where she could dress up, a fancy breakfast (New York Style Cheesecake French Toast with Strawberries and Whipped Cream) at the iconic Highland Diner, painting at a ceramic shop in Spencerport, carousel rides at Charlotte Beach and the malls, and the Ukrainian festival to watch the dancers.

We frequently went to the playground near the Walmart on Howard Road and Chili Avenue. Amanda didn't want to go down the slide without me, so I went for it. Unfortunately, I got an elbow brush-burn that bled. When my friends asked me about my bandaged elbow, I just said, "Playground injury." They all laughed. At the Black Creek playground, there was an *extremely* tanned mother with her daughter on the swings. Amanda asked loudly why she was black and her little girl was white. I whisked her out of there and explained that the mother was very tan.

Whenever we went to Petsmart or the Lollipop Farm store at the Greece mall, we'd always go to the pets that were available for adoption. She is allergic to cats, but that didn't stop her from petting them. She has volunteered at her local vet on occasion, as well.

When she got into a soccer league at 5 years old, they happened to play a game on Jeff's birthday, July 16.

Afterwards, the team went to the Byrne Dairy on Chili Avenue and Union Street for ice cream, where the little girls sang "Happy Birthday" to Jeff. It was very touching and brought tears to my eyes.

A few years ago, Amanda and I walked the pier in Seabreeze in Irondequoit, NY. After we finished walking the pier and enjoying the sand, we headed back to my car. Suddenly we heard a cry for help. It was coming from the Porta Potty! There was a man stuck inside and he had been in there for quite a while in the hot summer sun. He was banging on the door and screaming for help, so we yelled that we were on our way. We told him to push as Amanda and I pulled. The door was wedged shut, but finally we were able to get it open. He was eternally grateful. We did our good deed for the day!

Some of my babysitting days were spent quietly at her house. She would swing on her tree swing, we made arts and crafts, played with the Wii (once, I beat her in dance moves!), had picnic lunches on the porch, visited her friend Italia and they played with their dolls. We played board games, looked at YouTube videos, played with Barbies and her American Girl doll, played "school," used chalk to make roads on the driveway and raced Matchbox cars, took bike rides and walks, and I'd watch her swim in her neighbor's pool where the kids had fun.

When she'd come to my house, I always brought out Eric's old Fisher Price toys (Village, Camper, Airport, and Service Station). We would play for hours. Sometimes I'd fill the kiddie pool and we'd play with Barbie and Ken in the pool. She stayed overnight a few times, but her cat allergy made her very uncomfortable. She did love my cats, although she pulled Natasha's tail one time. Natasha shrieked but never tried to scratch or bite her.

Every Thanksgiving the family would go out for dinner. One year, Eric, Hanne, Amanda, Marcia, Jeff and I dined at Keenan's in Irondequoit and they didn't have any whipped cream for the pie. So, the next year, when the pie was served and the waitress left our table, I brought out a can of Reddi-Whip from my purse. Eric, Amanda, and I smothered our pumpkin pie in whipped cream. When a waiter walked by, he did a double-take! We all laughed really hard. I made it a tradition to always stash Reddi-Whip in my purse so that we always had plenty.

When Amanda was small, I tried to explain to her that she wasn't just of German ancestry like her Oma and Opa; she was also Polish, Ukrainian, and English. When I told her that Poland was next door to Germany, she looked at her neighbor's house. Haha. Amanda is also a "Daughter of the American Revolution," as she has ancestors on Jeff's side who came over on the *Mayflower* and the *Anne,* and also several who fought in the Revolution. In fact, one great grandparent can be traced back to Knights and Ladies of the English court to the year 800 A.D.! I created an Ancestry tree for our family and I hope she will maintain it at some point.

As Amanda grew older, she'd bring her bow and arrow and target shoot in our backyard, fly a kite, play bocce and ladderball, and also basketball using my neighbor's hoop.

Jeff and I go to her high school functions now—her soccer league, cross-country meets, track, chorus, band concerts, and award ceremonies.

Now that she's 16 and I obviously no longer need to babysit, I fondly look back upon those times and wish that I could do them all over again. Amanda was the daughter I never had. The greatest joy in my life. She has grown up to be a beautiful young woman, and I love her very much. I hope she will remember all the fun things we did together and think of me with the same fondness. I will always watch over her, even from "the other side."

My Year of Adventure

WHEN I RETIRED, I DECIDED IT was going to be my Year of Adventure (2004). I bought a book called "Take a Hike" by Rich and Sue Freeman and went on several of the trails, including Helmer Nature Center, Springdale Farms, Bay Trail, and others.

I was a little nervous hiking by myself, but I stayed aware of my surroundings at all times. On the late spring day that I walked the Bay Trail, I drove down Smith Road and looked for a place to park. I saw a wide dock which I assumed was part of the park and used for fishing and swimming. I parked my car a little further down the road and walked the trail. I loved being in the woods, hearing all the birds singing and seeing the ferns on the forest floor.

I kept thinking about the dock in the park, so when I got home, I called my sister Marcia and told her I had a surprise. I asked her to pack up a folding chair, comic books, magazines, or whatever reading material she wanted and be ready early the next morning. I picked her up with all her gear and we took a short drive to the park.

I was surprised that no one was using the dock, but happy we had it all to ourselves. We set up our folding chairs and got out our *Little Lulu, Donald Duck,* and *Dennis the*

Menace comic books. It was so serene out there and we watched boats go by and soaked up the sun.

Suddenly a carp jumped out of the water! Then two, then three, then more! We screamed! They were in a frenzy, flopping around and fighting, splashing us in the process. We screamed again because we (and our comic books) were getting wet! Boaters were staring at us, not knowing why we were screaming and laughing.

After two hours or so, we had enough sun and packed up our gear and left. We hoped we could come back again.

I did drive down there again during the summer, but this time there was someone on the dock. They yelled at me for parking near the dock and said it was private property! (OMG! I honestly didn't know!) I told them what a lovely spot they had, and moved on. Marcia and I never went back, but we will always remember the day we sat on that dock. (Apologies to the owner!)

* * * * *

Even before my year of adventure, I enjoyed hiking in the woods or near creeks and ponds. One year during June, two of my friends from Kodak, Mary-Helen Maginn and Judy Dougherty, and I decided to check out Mendon Ponds. We heard that chickadees would feed right out of your hand. So, we brought some seed and walked the Devil's Bathtub Trail. We didn't see a single chickadee but we did see mosquitoes—thousands of them—and they all wanted to feast on us! We screamed and went running like banshees out of there!

The next time we got together was for a Kodak team outing at Powder Mills Park. *"Haha, mosquitoes, you aren't going to get me this time!"* I said. Mary-Helen brought some Avon mosquito repellent which I lathered on my face—too late to discover it was OIL. My entire face was covered in oil. My glasses wouldn't stay up. When the oil got into my eyes, it burned, and my sight was blurred, yet I had to climb the steep trail with my co-workers. Mary-Helen couldn't stop laughing. Dang! I did myself in. Didn't get a single mosquito bite, though.

In more recent years, I loved going birding with my friends Judy Caysinger, Mary-Helen, and Renee Nobles. We would go to a lesser-known trail, which we called the Firehouse Trail, since it was next to the Lakeshore Fire Department on Long Pond Road near Edgemere. Every May and June we'd walk the level trail around ponds and wetlands and look for warblers. Most of these birds flew high in the trees, so we always ended up with "warbler neck," from looking straight up with binoculars. My favorite bird sighting was that of a Scarlet Tanager who sang for us for twenty minutes in a lower tree. My favorite warbler was the Blackburnian Warbler, with its blazing orange color. I'd feel so blessed if I saw one close-up in a shrub. We also went to Northampton Park and Hamlin Beach State Park and saw Eastern Bluebirds, my favorite bird of all time, for their brilliant blue color and beautiful song.

About once a year, my sister Patty and I went to Bluebird Haven in Victor near her house and we'd walk the trail through the woods then out into the open where there were many bluebird boxes. Sometimes we'd see Eastern Bluebirds and sometimes we didn't. On one excursion, we were disappointed that we didn't see any. We went back to her house and there, on the deck, was a bluebird! Another trail near her house was the Monkey-Run Trail, where a bluebird serenaded us for such a long time that we had to move on.

I was surprised that I didn't get many bluebirds around my house on Bald Eagle Drive, although I had seen them a few times on the wires. However, I often saw Tree and Barn Swallows, Purple Martins, Hummingbirds, Baltimore Orioles, Orchard Orioles, Red-Winged Blackbirds, Rose-Breasted Grosbeaks, Red-Bellied Woodpeckers, Northern Flickers, hundreds of migrating Bluejays every May, Robins, Tufted Titmice, Chickadees, Juncos, Snow Buntings, White-Crowned, Song, and Fox Sparrows, Goldfinches, Cedar Waxwings, Killdeer, Yellow Warblers, Catbirds, Mockingbirds, an occasional Indigo Bunting, Snowy Owls, Kingfishers, Green Herons, Great Blue Herons, Turkey Vultures, Mergansers, Loons, and, yes, Bald Eagles. I pray that I will see an Eastern Meadowlark again some day. Their numbers are dwindling.

The Lucid Dream

EVERYONE HAS LUCID DREAMS NOW and then. Some people have more than others. I remember my dreams quite often, but one dream stands out above the rest.

I was in a deep sleep. Suddenly a voice was calling me in my subconscious. "Ella! Ella!" it cried out. It was my mother's voice. She had been dead for many years, but I still recognized the sound of her voice.

"Ella, guess who I met?" she squealed with excitement. "William Holden!"

*Lucid Dream of
My Mom Meeting
Actor William Holden
in Heaven.*

*(Photo: No copyright
infringement intended.)*

I awoke with a start. It was so real, that I had to look around my room, expecting Mom to be there. But I could not see or sense anyone in the shadows.

Was it a dream? Was it my imagination? I'll never know, at least in this life. This short dream seemed very, very real.

I was a bit confused by her excitement, though. I knew that William Holden was a movie star from the past, but I had no idea what he looked like or which movies he starred in. In fact, I knew nothing about him at all.

The next time I got together with my sisters Marcia and Patty, I told them about the dream. Marcia said, "Oh yeah. Mom loved William Holden. Didn't you ever see him in that episode of *I Love Lucy* where he played himself?"

I was sure I had seen all of the *I Love Lucy* episodes, but I didn't remember him. Marcia informed me that, in the episode, Lucy was in Hollywood and went into the Brown Derby, a celebrity hangout, for lunch, where she encountered movie stars William Holden and Eve Arden. As Lucy's show typically progressed, she accidentally bumped the waiter who hit Holden in the face with a cream pie! It sounded vaguely familiar to me, but as a child watching *Lucy*, I wouldn't have known who he was. I hadn't seen *Sunset Boulevard* or any of his other movies at that point.

The other thing that bothered me about the dream was that, throughout the 50s and 60s, Mom was crazy about Perry Como. He's all I ever heard about. So, I wondered why she met William Holden and not Perry!

It's great that Mom got to meet William (and I truly believe she did). Now I have to wonder if Dad ever met Dinah Shore and why he didn't wake me up to tell me!

The Sloopers

BACK IN OCTOBER 2004, THE Historical Society erected a plaque at the corner of my street (Bald Eagle Drive and Norway Road in the town of Kendall, New York) and held a ceremony for its dedication. I attended along with 15 (or so) others from the neighborhood and town.

They started out with a brief introduction by Joette Knapp (Kendall Town Historian), a prayer from the Lutheran

Historical Marker dedicated to the Norway Colony,
the first settlement of the Norwegians in the United States
on the corner of Norway Road and Bald Eagle Drive.

minister, the singing of the Norwegian national anthem, then "My Country, 'Tis of Thee," followed by the story of The Sloopers from a man named Bill Andrews, then a closing prayer.

Here's what I remember of the story of The Sloopers (Bill had a copy of a HUGE book about their journey).

A group of Norwegians were interested in coming to this country during the Napoleonic Wars. It was also a time of religious and economic unrest. They were befriended by a group of Quakers who owned the land in Kendall and who encouraged the Norwegians to settle here. In 1825, 52 Norwegian men, women, and children set sail in a 250-sq. ft. boat called *The Restauration*, which, in essence, gave each person 2.5 feet of room. Their first port was England, where the English proposed a trade. The English promised food for their journey in trade for a barrel of whiskey. The English took the whiskey and the next morning told them to leave port or be arrested, as this particular trade for whiskey was illegal.

The Norwegians left port without the extra food and headed for the Madeira Islands. Along the way they discovered a barrel floating in the ocean and, lo and behold, it was filled with wine. Apparently, all the men became inebriated and didn't raise their flag as they neared Madeira. They were assumed to be either pirates or a plague ship and were about to be fired upon (with cannon) when one of the women onboard started flapping her skirt over the bow. After some discussion, the Madeirans concluded that they weren't dangerous and allowed them to port.

During their ocean voyage a baby was born, bringing the number of people to 53. Their next stop was New York City, where the captain, Lars Olsen Hellend, was promptly arrested and the boat impounded for having too many people aboard a ship so small (only 16 people were allowed by law). The Sloopers, as they were called, went on without their captain by way of steamship up the Hudson River to Albany, where they then followed the Erie Canal to Holley, NY. (They were the first immigrant group to travel the newly opened Erie Canal.) They walked through nine miles of forest to the shore of Lake Ontario, where they settled in the area from Norway Road to Kendall Road. Meanwhile, the Quakers in NYC raised enough money to free the captain from jail and petitioned John Quincy Adams to pardon the captain and allow the boat to be sold so that the money could be used by the Norwegian colony. They were expecting to obtain $4,000 for the ship but only received $400, a terrible disappointment. Because the Erie Canal was frozen, the captain decided to ice skate all the way from Albany to Holley, a distance record still unbeaten to this day.

One man in the colony, Jacob Anderson Slogvik, who was 18 years old at the time, married and farmed the land that is now the corner of Norway Road and Bald Eagle Drive. He had 40 acres, or about six properties at the time. After a brutal Kendall winter in 1834, many of the colony moved west to the Fox River Settlement in Illinois and Jacob moved his family as well. He stayed there for a while, but later moved to Iowa (where they became Mormons), and later still to Napa Valley, CA. There he had a 400-acre dairy farm. He had a huge boulder shipped from Norway to his farm in CA and had it engraved with an image of *The Restauration* and a dedication.

The Kendall Town Historian said that there are still several descendants of The Sloopers in Orleans County.

Martha Stewart's People

AT THE END OF JUNE 2005, I saw an article saying Martha Stewart, American retail executive businesswoman, writer, and television personality, was looking for the "worst cooks in America," a title that would easily fit me, for a reality TV series. The person who made the most progress and prepared a meal without a hitch would win a cash prize.

I wrote to the e-mail address given in the article and told them why I might be the worst cook in America.

I wrote,

―――――――――――――

"Dear Martha,

"When I heard that you were looking for the worst cook, I knew I could be the one. Unfortunately.

"After my honeymoon in 1968 and the first morning of bliss in our new apartment, I decided to make breakfast for my darling husband Jeff. I put on the automatic coffee pot and started bacon and eggs, just like my Mom did for my Dad. Suddenly there was an acrid smell and my husband quickly unplugged the coffee pot. He was in shock. "You forgot to put water in this!" he exclaimed. I asked, "Oh, I didn't know I had

221

to. Where does it come from?" Jeff settled for a glass of Tang.

"Sometime later, I received a cake recipe from my landlady who cooked for a local school. I bought self-rising flour by mistake. What difference would it make? And I didn't know it was enough to feed THE SCHOOL. My cake pan overflowed in the oven and it looked like an episode from I Love Lucy—dough everywhere. I didn't stop baking it; I just kept transferring the mixture to new pans until the oven was full. We tried eating the result; but it was so hard and salty, we ended up burying the cakes in the back yard. I thought I heard Jeff praying.

"Some other failures occurred when I didn't have an ingredient and substituted something from my pantry. The herbs and spices were way off base, ruining everything. I wish I knew more about flavoring food because I'm obviously clueless. And there are three rules in my house: don't give me power tools and appliances, matches, or knives, because I could be a danger to myself.

"Surprisingly, my son and husband survived 37 years of my cooking failures. My husband cooks whenever he can, saving me embarrassment and dinner-time arguments. My son started eating out at 16 until he married (and she's a wonderful cook). He lives only 40 minutes away and I can understand why he doesn't visit often. When I prepare an infrequent meal for his family, I am so disorganized that the menu items are never synchronized or prepared on time. They may start eating their meat before *everything else is ready. I can't seem to find enough time for preparing everything, entertaining them, and meeting their immediate needs. I need help!*

"It's also discouraging that my kitchen isn't very efficient or effective for preparing a meal and I can't afford a new one since I recently retired. But I still have 30 good years in me; I'm ready to learn to cook. I'd love to surprise my family with an exquisite, well-prepared meal. Maybe my husband's prayers would be answered!"

———————————

On July 3, Martha's "people" called me on the phone. They asked if I could submit a video, shooting a cooking disaster in my kitchen, and ship the video to them by the next day, July 4.

I said I'd try, but in 2005, you had to have a video camera to shoot a video. My flip phone didn't have that capability, much less the capability to e-mail a video. You had to ship a VHS cartridge via Federal Express. And I didn't have time to rent a video camera either. Besides, how could I ship anything on the Fourth of July? I was expecting company for the holiday and had a lot of preparations—grocery shopping, cooking side dishes, cleaning, etc. (Jeff was going to grill the hots and hamburgers outside.)

I thought about getting a slab of fresh salmon and cooking it in the microwave. I knew it would blow up because, well, I tried that before. And what a mess it makes!! It would have made a great kitchen disaster video.

Alas, I gave up because I just didn't time to turn it around in one day—and a holiday, at that. But it was fun to tell all my friends that Martha Stewart's "people" called me.

RV Disaster

In July 2006 we began renovations on our Bald Eagle Drive home. The Bropsts, friends of Robert and Heather Stone, our builders, allowed us to rent their RV for the duration. The Town of Kendall permitted us to park the RV in our driveway and live in it, as long as it was removed immediately afterwards. We anticipated that to be Labor Day, but construction took longer than expected, and we were still in the RV through October. The permit actually ran out in September, but the Town said they would look the other way unless a neighbor complained. No one did.

During demolition, we parked the RV across the street in front of the pole barn. Eric, Hanne, and Amanda came to check it out. As we were inside the RV, we all turned our heads for a split second as Amanda pushed on the screen door. Unfortunately, it wasn't locked and she took a tumble down the three steps to the rocky driveway. She cried, but was otherwise unharmed. We did a thorough check right down to her teeth. I was grateful that I had had the foresight to place a rubber mat by the stairs so her fall was softened a bit.

While the RV was parked across the street, it had no electricity so we couldn't really live in it. It was fine to sit at the kitchen table and eat, but we needed lights and outlets for everyday appliances. The bedroom in the house was untouched in the demolition, so we thought we would sleep there as long as possible and be close to the bathroom and our clothes.

When the builders knocked out all the windows in the house except for the bedroom, we couldn't stop the inevitable onslaught of insects that came in, particularly at night. The first night was annoying, but tolerable. The second night, I awoke to an insect gnawing on my butt. "Yow!" I yelled and jumped up to turn on the lights. I threw back the sheets, and there were not one, not two, but at least what appeared to be a dozen Japanese beetles in our bed. Big, red beetles with pinchers. They were not just on the sheets and blanket, but they had managed to crawl between the mattress and the mattress cover as well. That was it. I had to sleep in the RV. I left Jeff to fend for himself, grabbed an old comforter and my pillow, and trotted out to the RV in pitch darkness.

When we moved the RV to the paved driveway next to the house, Robert hooked up the electricity so that we could run air conditioning and plug in our appliances. However, the RV's a/c blew a fuse and left everyone without power. Since he couldn't run his saw, Robert had to leave and buy what was necessary to fix it. After several hours, Robert replaced the fuse and we finally had all the conveniences of home.

You don't want to know what my electricity bill was like during August. Yikes! Using electricity for the RV was only part of it; the builders also had all their equipment going. The drywall guys used large heat lamps and fans throughout

SEARCHING FOR SERENITY IN MY CRAZY LIFE

the house. Plus, for a full week, I had used a heat gun to remove ancient commercial tile squares from the laundry room floor, piece by tiny piece. It was brittle but cemented to last forever. While I was doing that, Jeff was using a sledge hammer on the ceramic tiles in the hallway (also cemented) and had to light the area with a table lamp plugged into an outlet in the second bedroom.

By mid-October, it was getting pretty darned cold at night. The RV had electric heat only in the front part of the vehicle where I slept, but the bedroom, where Jeff slept, had none. Yet, I was the one who was finding this whole experience of RV living a bit tedious. I was anxious to sleep back in my own bed. (P.S. Real windows had been installed.)

The problem was, the house wasn't quite ready for occupancy. After Robert and Heather were finishing up with new moldings throughout and a wall of beadboard in the master bedroom, we still had other contractors on the job. Penny, the painter, had some last-minute work; Rusty, the Pergo installer, had to lay the flooring; Rich, the carpet guy, had to replace the carpet in the bedroom and to lay vinyl in the laundry room; Big Ash had to re-install our propane stove in the living room; Mike, the heating contractor, had to remove the old oil tank; Hometowne Energy had to install the propane tanks and convert the range to propane; Mike also had to start up and test the new heating system; and last but not least, the countertops had to be installed in the kitchen and laundry rooms (a story in itself).

In addition to the contractors, I had decided to spruce up the bathroom myself. After all, we had a bathroom in the RV and a new powder room off the computer room. Jeff and I removed the large sheet mirror, the lighting fixture, the

227

exhaust fan over the shower, and all the moldings. It was my job to remove the wallpaper, but my tried-and-true method (of an application of hot water covered by a large lawn bag) didn't work. As the wallpaper came down, so did the drywall, in large patches. And, apparently, a former owner *glued* all the wallpaper seams. Robert, Heather, and Penny shook their heads and felt sorry for me. Since it wasn't part of their contract, I was on my own. They suggested hiring the drywall guys to re-mud the room, but after a very bad experience with all our ceilings, I said, "No way." If you looked at the ceilings, you would see a dimple wherever there was a screw, and Robert and Heather pointed fingers at the drywall guys, while the drywall guys pointed fingers at Robert. Robert ended up patching every dimple and Penny had to touch up the paint. In the computer room, Penny repainted the entire ceiling.

But back to the bathroom... While we had a new powder room in the computer room, the main bathroom housed the only shower (no tub). It took two weeks to get all the wallpaper down, then on a day when no contractors were in the house, I decided to mud the walls. Robert had a large bucket of mud that would not be used again, so I helped myself to it. I had watched plenty of do-it-yourself shows on TV and felt confident I could do this.

Once I finished, I was pretty pleased with the result. I knew I had to re-do a small wall above the shower stall because it didn't dry smooth, and the tight corner next to the vanity and the spot for the tissue holder didn't look that great, so I had to redo those, too. But first I had to sand, and sand I did for over an hour the next morning. I was covered from head to toe with drywall dust. When I blinked you could see my brown eyes pop, but the rest of me looked like a ghost. The entire bathroom was coated in the fine dust, too, making it totally unusable. *"Thank God for the RV,"* I thought.

I had been listening to the weather reports for October 12, 2006, and a front was expected to pass through around 11 a.m. and then turn sharply colder. Rain and even several inches of wet snow were in the forecast. I started to panic because I hadn't replanted my hostas, my potted lavender, and two new ornamental grasses for the front of the house. I figured I was a walking disaster with all the drywall dust anyway, what's a little dirt? I'd just shower in the RV afterwards.

The hostas went in easily, although the clay soil was cold, wet, and sloppy. I started to dig holes for the lavender and grasses but ran into an enormous obstacle. A little more digging revealed a huge maple tree root that extended right along the line of the garden bed. I called my neighbor, Steve Maley, on the phone and asked if he had a small saw or axe that I could borrow to cut the root. He was baking a pie but promised to come over as soon as possible.

Steve showed up and offered to cut the root for me in three places. I pulled while he sawed and we finally removed a portion of the root and dug three holes large enough for my plants. It had started to rain, and then snow. The drywall dust was now sticking to my skin, hair, and clothes, and the clay soil covered the knees of my jeans and embedded into my fingernails. I wasn't just dirty; I was filthy.

I went into the house and grabbed some clean underwear, jeans, and shirt and headed over to the RV for a hot shower. The rain mixed with snow was falling steadily, accumulating into a slushy mess on the grass. Once inside the privacy of the RV, I removed all my clothes at the door (I didn't want to drag mud through the RV) and walked naked toward the shower. I thought to myself, *"Darn. I probably should have peed while I was in the house. Well, I'll just use the toilet here in the RV."*

Up to this point we hadn't used the toilet much because the RV's holding tank was small. The more you used the toilet, the more you had to hook up the RV's sewer hose to the septic tank, and that took two people. We made it a practice to empty the "gray" and "black" water once a week, on the weekend. This was Tuesday so the tank was still fairly empty.

After I relieved myself, I pushed the handle to flush. After emptying, the water level started to rise in the toilet bowl. It wasn't supposed to do that. It suddenly occurred to me that the toilet was going to overflow. "Oh, no!" I screamed, and flushed it again. Once again, the water began to rise. "AHHH!" I screamed out of frustration and fear. There I was, buck naked, and the only shut-off was at the water spigot on the side of the house. That meant I had to go outside. And FAST.

I grabbed my clean shirt and threw it on over my head. Flushed again. I grabbed my clean jeans and struggled into them. Flushed again. Then I was worried that the holding tank would overflow and I KNEW there was No. 2 down there. I couldn't let that happen. I RAN through the RV and outside in my bare feet, holding my jeans shut (I didn't have time to zipper them and hoped no one would see me). I slipped on the cold, slushy grass, and fell face first into the mud. I got up, looked around to see if anyone had been watching me, and continued to run to the house. I shut off the spigot and ran back to the RV door. Once inside the RV, I ran back to the bathroom, where I flushed the toilet just as the water teetered at the rim. It didn't refill. I had averted disaster. Whew!

Now I had another dilemma. I couldn't use the RV shower because I couldn't turn the water back on. I had no choice but to use the shower in the house. I looked at the state of the RV. The entire floor was covered in wet, muddy footprints. Both pairs of jeans and shirts were filthy. I didn't have a new washer and dryer installed yet. I desperately needed a shower, as my face was still coated with drywall dust which was hardening and my hands and feet were muddy. However, I'd have to clean the drywall dust from the entire bathroom before attempting to shower.

Once again without shoes, I went outside in the rain and snow and into the house. I figured I'd just throw on my cotton nightgown to clean the bathroom, so I dumped the dirty clothes on the floor, donned the nightgown, grabbed a bucket and sponge, and climbed into the shower stall. Suddenly, I thought I heard noises in the house. I listened, and sure enough, someone was there! Inside the house! I had no choice but to confront them in my nightgown. I couldn't even make it into the bedroom. When I emerged from the bathroom, I discovered that the contractors, Robert and Heather, had let themselves in and were inspecting the most recent work.

"Uh, hi," I said. "Sorry about my appearance. I was just cleaning drywall dust in the bathroom." I must have looked like a crazy person, covered in dust and mud from head to toe and my hair all askew. I didn't want to tell them that

I might have broken the RV toilet, but sooner or later, I would have to call their friends, the Bropsts, who owned the RV.

Once they were gone, I finished my task and took a hot shower. After I found clean clothes to wear, I cleaned up the mud that I had tracked through the RV. Then I called Joe Bropst to tell him about the toilet. He came over and looked at the problem. It necessitated a trip to the home improvement store, which would take about an hour. When he returned with parts, he discovered they weren't going to take care of the problem and he had to make another hour trip. I felt very bad, but he took it in stride. It was after 5 p.m. by the time he had the toilet working again. He and Jeff emptied the holding tank and we were back in business. By that time, I decided that I would start using the house bathroom again so I wouldn't have a repeat of my RV disaster.

Bell's Palsy

WOW, SOMETIMES YOU don't know what hits you. Or why.

For a few weeks, I had bitched to myself about not being able to read the cable guide on TV. I blamed my new glasses. I also had to have an eye test to renew my license, and I chose to do it at my eye doctor's rather than at the DMV. I was blinded by the lighted chart when the technician turned off the room lights. I strained my eyes to see the letters and she had to try twice to get a satisfactory response.

Also, for a few weeks, I also noticed that, when I sang along to some country music, I favored my right side. I thought it was odd and actually looked at myself in the mirror with curiosity. I had thought to myself, "Gee, I'd hate to have a stroke and look like this all the time."

On Thursday, April 9, 2009, I met friends Judy Caysinger, Mary-Helen Maginn, and Renee Nobles for dinner at The Garland House. We wanted to do something nice for Renee, who had just lost her mother. While I was there, I started to get an ear ache under the left ear. Over the next four days, I took aspirin, then allergy medication, then sinus medication, and put in drops for ear pain. I decided that if it continued through Monday, I'd call the doctor on Tuesday, in case I had an ear infection.

Then, on Monday, April 13, I was babysitting my granddaughter at her house when my lips felt numb, like I had Novocaine. I felt fine, and my mental faculties were sharp, so I drove home and made dinner. But when I went to eat dinner, I was sloppy, like I was drooling. I got on the computer and looked up the signs of stroke. I fit a few of them but not all of them. What the heck was going on?

In the middle of the night I got up to have a glass of water. I put the glass to my mouth and it ended up coming out as quickly as I put it in. My mouth was totally awry. That scared the crap out of me. I wrote a note to Jeff, in case I really was having a stroke and might even kick the bucket. I took a shower, woke up Jeff, and called Dr. Meloni, who said I needed to get to the Emergency Room asap. My doctor was concerned that hospital in Brockport might not have the latest equipment, so Jeff chose to drive me to Rochester General Hospital (after he took a shower).

Jeff dropped me off at the ER entrance, which was under construction, while he went to find a parking spot. There was no one there to greet me so I just walked in and followed the arrows. Surprisingly, no one else was in the ER waiting. At the desk, I told the girl that I thought I had had a stroke. She said, "Who had a stroke?" I said me. She immediately ushered me to a chair, where they took all my vital signs and asked me questions like, what year is it—I had to count up from 1999 in my head! Good thing she didn't ask me the name of the President. I might have said Bush or Clinton. Obama did not register.

By the time Jeff arrived in the ER, I was already in a bed. Linda put the blood pressure cuff on me and started an IV, which I never got. Then the shift changed. Amy was the new tech and Kingsley was an aide. The ER doctor, Chuck, took me for a CT scan, which he said was "fabulous." He also checked my ears and said they weren't infected. Since all my vitals were perfect, even my blood pressure and sugar, and my CT scan was fine, he said I didn't have a stroke. What I had was Bell's palsy. I had heard the term, but didn't know what it was.

Doctors aren't really sure what causes Bell's. It could be a direct injury to the facial nerve, a virus related to chickenpox, Lyme disease, a badly placed Novocaine shot, or anything else that would cause inflammation of the facial nerve. Bell's usually begins by pain under the ear. It "freezes" one side of your face and you look like a stroke victim, with a drooping bottom eye lid and a wry mouth. I couldn't blink my left eye, no matter what I told my brain to do. They gave me three cotton eye patches to wear and said I would have to wear one for several weeks so that the cornea wouldn't dry out. Chuck also wrote a script for 6 days of Prednisone, an anti-inflammatory.

After they fed me breakfast (I brought along a breakfast bar for Jeff), and all the release papers were signed, I was discharged. We stopped to fill the prescription on the way home. Jeff dropped me off and went to work. I had to buy natural tears and a permanent eye patch so I drove to Tops with one eye. I had to get the pharmacist to help me, since I couldn't read the packaging on any boxes. Later, I made an appointment to see Dr. Meloni in two days, who concurred with the diagnosis of the ER doctor. By the time I saw my doctor, I could close both my eyes together, which was an improvement. Whoo-hoo.

During all this, Eric and Hanne treated me and Jeff to a night in Toronto, complete with dinner at Ruth's Chris Steak House and tickets to see the Andre Rieu concert. The four of us were in the nose-bleed section of the stadium and everyone on stage looked like an ant. (Good thing for movie screens!) But it was walking up and down the stairs to our seats with one eye that caused the most issue. They made me dizzy.

I suppose things could have been worse, but Bell's can knock you for a loop. You're exhausted, you can't focus or read, you have to rely on your good eye, which for me was my lazy eye. After a while, I was cross-eyed. Eating and especially drinking were challenging. Driving was almost impossible the first week. But it did get better. After 16 days, I was about 60% better. My smile wasn't quite right yet, I still couldn't squeeze my left eye shut, and my right ear felt plugged, but I could read better and feel human again.

The lesson here is, question everything, no matter how slight or how odd. Don't waste time getting to the ER. And enjoy life; you never know how short it will be.

Oh yeah, be prepared to pay a $1600 ER bill too.

Meeting An American Idol

I WAS FEELING SORRY FOR MYSELF on August 8, 2009, because I wasn't able to get in to the WPXY Invitation-Only Meet and Greet with *American Idol* Runner-Up, Blake Lewis. I had previously missed out on meeting David Cook, who was my favorite singer EVER on Idol.

When Blake first appeared on Idol, I wasn't sure how ready America was to accept a beatboxer, especially *American Idol* fans who are typically pop oriented. But Blake was the runner-up that season and I voted for him every week. There was something riveting about his style, and when I purchased his first CD, I couldn't put it down. In fact, I play it often and never get tired of it. His lyrics are very personal, so I related to it even though I might not be "living" it.

When I heard that Blake was coming to Rochester I called WPXY and was disappointed that I couldn't attend Blake's meet and greet, performance, and interview without an invitation. I also called 13WHAM since Blake was due to perform live on their morning show on August 9. Channel 13 told me that, while there would be no official meet and greet for fans, I could come to the parking lot and greet him myself. I checked Twitter in the morning, and Blake hadn't gone to sleep until 2:30 a.m. I hmm'd and haw'd, feeling silly about driving an hour in rush-hour traffic for the outside chance of seeing Blake in person. (Me, a 61-year-old grandma!) I didn't know if there would be hordes of fans—all young, hip, thin, and tattooed girls, screaming; I hoped I would be the only fan there. And I was!

I paced the parking lot for twenty minutes, and when he pulled in, my heart was beating out of my chest. I got a few shots with my Kodak digital camera, then, when he approached, I asked him for his autograph on my CD insert. After he signed it, I asked Blake if one of his band members could take a picture of us. He was very sweet and, with a big smile, said "Sure!" Then he had to go inside the studio.

American Idol Runner-Up, Season 6, Blake Lewis
and Me at WHAM ABC Channel 13.

I asked a 13WHAM worker if I could watch the taping, but they said they weren't set up for that, so I had to watch it online. When he made reference to the House of Guitars, I almost fell over! I told him to check out HOG since he was interested in vinyl albums, and he listened and took me up on that!

I couldn't stop smiling—it was a really special day to meet an Idol! It wasn't just "serenity"; I was on Cloud 9!

A year or so later, I entered Blake's contest to say why I was a big fan. I wrote about meeting him in the 13WHAM parking lot and how I felt as a 61-year-old fan. What I didn't know was that his mother was reading the entries and picking two winners. I was the second winner! I won a t-shirt for his second album and an autographed picture. Sweet!

* * * * *

In March 2016, Patty and I bought tickets to see *American Idol* Winner, David Cook perform in Buffalo. We stood outside for an hour in the cold, then another hour inside (in a mosh pit) before the concert, then three hours for the concert. It was extremely uncomfortable to stand for five hours, but I would do it again to hear him perform.

Saying Goodbye to Mickey

JEFF AND I RAN INTO MY BROTHER Mickey (Mike) at Best Buy in Greece, NY, in May of 2010, he told us he was buying a Mother's Day gift for his kids, Alyssa and Michael, to give to their mom, Jill. He also revealed to us that he needed surgery. They were going to do laparoscopic surgery to remove a kidney. First, though, he wanted to take his kids to Disney World and then he and Jill would go to a Daughtry concert, his favorite band. He knew this surgery would not be good.

I wanted to be at the hospital before they took him to the OR, but he had other plans for me. He saw his kids off on their school buses and told them he loved them and would see them soon, but he knew it might not go that way. He asked me to be at his house to get the kids off the buses and bring them to the hospital, well into his surgery time. I also picked up Marcia; Patty came later. Around 6:30 p.m., Mickey was still in surgery so I took Alyssa and Michael back home and stayed with them until Jill arrived at midnight. She told me that Mickey went into intensive care and would be staying in the hospital for about 5 days.

The next day, Mickey was semi-conscious, barely recognized us, but gave me a little wave. Then, in the middle of the night, he took a turn for the worse. Jill called me at 2:45 a.m. saying that we needed to get to the hospital to say our goodbyes. I threw on some clothes and raced to her house in Hilton to pick her up. We got to the hospital but he was no longer conscious, and hanging on to life. The doctor said he needed emergency surgery to remove a clot. He might not survive.

Mickey did survive, but he required a ventilator, dialysis, and at least 12 bags of medicine. It was awful to see him like that, and the situation was dire. I went back to Jill's house and cleaned their powder room and kitchen for her parents' visit, all in the name of love for my brother.

We expected to be called in the middle of the next night, but the call didn't come until about 7:30 a.m. I went to the hospital alone (Jill's parents drove her), wondering if I'd make it in time. After a third surgery attempt, they couldn't do any more for him. Mickey passed away at 3:50 p.m. on July 23, 2010, with me, his daughter Shannon, and Jill in the room.

At the wake, many of his friends showed up as well as the Civil War re-enactors. It was actually a joyful reunion, and Mickey would have loved it.

At the service, his friends spoke about their friendship with Mickey. They described him as the kindest, most generous person, but also who was never afraid to do something absolutely ridiculous, all in the name of laughter. At Watkins Glen, Dave Taney said he dove into a mud hole in his skivvies, giving him the name Mudman. Another time, they threw coins at a flasher from the 5th story of the Taft Hotel in NYC, which ended with a police visit. Patty's eulogy talked about growing up with Mickey and his antics; I spoke as his older sister; his oldest daughter Shannon also gave a heartfelt speech.

But the one who impressed us most was his 8-year-old son, Michael. When the adults finished their eulogies, the Episcopal priest started back to the podium when little Michael stood up. Rev. Hill kindly ushered him to the podium. You could barely see the top of his head. No one in the room moved or even breathed.

He spoke from the heart:

"My name is Michael, and I am Mike's son. The last time I saw my daddy was on Tuesday before he went into the hospital. He walked me to the school bus, and gave me a big hug and said, 'I love you. I'll see you tomorrow.' Last year my daddy took me to the Hilton Carnival and we saw all the lights and the rides. It was really beautiful and I had a good time. Now my daddy is up in heaven watching us. I'm going to miss him very much."

The entire room was sobbing. His speech was so honest, so eloquent. It touched all of our hearts. Mickey would have been so proud. In fact, I know he was there and I know he was proud.

* * * * *

A little about the life of Mickey. He was a klutzy kid and was teased often for being the only person who fell UP the stairs. However, the day after my wedding, he fell DOWN on the driveway and broke his front teeth.

We thought he would grow up to be a salesman because he was always thinking up ways to make a buck. One time he took discarded clay flower pots from the cemetery and

Grandma Littlebetter's back porch and went door to door selling them for a few cents each. He sold every one. And once he borrowed a bag of Dad's cement and went door to door asking neighbors if they wanted their sidewalks patched. Another time, he and Patty found money on tables at Charlie's corner bar after a fish fry—he REALLY thought he struck pay dirt. Mom was mortified that he took the waitress' tips and paid them back.

One of our favorite Mickey-isms happened at Thanksgiving when he was about nine. As the family sat around Mom's dining room table, and after everyone sneezed (the Fedyk curse), Mickey decided to imitate a bat. He put his hands up to his armpits and fluttered them like a bat, complete with sound effects: "Pitchew, pitchew." Everyone laughed. We still imitate him whenever we see a bat or talk about that day.

Mickey was the ultimate character and should have been an actor. On Saturday morning, Mickey would watch *The Three Stooges* and could mimic Curly's "Woo, Nyuk" with remarkable skill. He even looked like Curly when he had a brush cut.

The House of Guitars lost one of its greatest advocates when Mickey passed away. Saying, "Hop, hop. Hop, hop," was like a secret code word among HOG patrons. And even when it wasn't Christmas, Mickey would enter your house like the Santa in *A Christmas Story,* and in his *slow*, deep voice, he'd bellow, "Ho! Ho! Ho!"

We both enjoyed *Star Trek,* but Mickey could recite almost every line from every episode. "Prepare to be assimilated. Resistance is futile."

He also emulated Homer on *The Simpsons* and, whenever he said, "D'oh!" everyone would laugh. A few of his favorite Homer quotes were:

- Doughnuts. Is there anything they can't do?
- Oh, so they have internet on computers now!

Halloween was a big deal for Mickey, too. He loved dressing up in outrageous costumes and, when we both lived in the city, he always came to our house on Halloween night with Shannon, both in costume. When he became involved with the Off-Monroe Players, he got into his roles and sang those Gilbert & Sullivan tunes with real gusto! The Civil War re-enactments were very important to him, too. Not only did he participate in them, but he read everything he could get his hands on about the war and individual soldiers, visited Gettysburg and other Civil War sites, and truly put himself in their boots.

He was a very patient and loving father to Shannon, Alyssa, Michael, Kaleigh, and his granddaughter Arianna. He was the techie in his family, too, always making sure Alyssa and Michael had their laptops in working order.

Mickey never lost his sense of humor, though, even on that day of the first surgery. When they were rolling his gurney down the hall to the Operating Room, he sang a bawdy tune at the top of his lungs, *"I love to go swimmin' with bow-legged women!"* that reflected his mischievous, sometimes comical life. It was so like Mickey. You go, Mickey!

And on day he died, he probably said to himself, "Beam me up, Scotty," and I'm sure he went straight to heaven.

Grandma Rides a Go-Kart

THE DAY DIDN'T EXACTLY TURN OUT the way I expected. I had to watch nine-year-old Amanda one last time before the end of summer 2012 and my plan was to take her to a miniature golf course either in Henrietta or Greece, NY. Hanne, Amanda's mom, had some BOGO coupons for The Clubhouse in Henrietta so that was the place to go.

Amanda didn't wake up until 9:30 a.m. About that time, the doorbell rang and it was her friend Arinae from next door. I told her that Amanda would be out later. When Amanda finally got up, the doorbell rang again and this time it was a Dan Fulmer installer wanting up put up shutters as the final touch on their siding job. Amanda and I waited until he finished and then she went outside on the tree swing. Eleven-year-old Arinae and her five-year-old brother Jaden came over to play. Amanda told them that we were going to play miniature golf and invited them! I admonished her that I didn't have the money to pay for everyone. The kids ran home and got $40 from their mother. I felt ambushed.

So, we all piled in my little Honda Civic, with all three kids in the back seat. Jaden used a booster seat and the two girls buckled up. I put on Amanda's Kidz Bop CD and the first song was Kelly Clarkson's "Stronger." Well, the ride was actually a lot of fun. The kids were belting out the song and we were all pumping our fists to the verse. Then they sang "Call Me Maybe," "Starships," and "Glad You Came." Cute little voices and they knew all the words, even Jaden!

When we got to The Clubhouse, they immediately wanted to go on the go-karts. The problem was Jaden was too small to go alone and had to ride with an adult—as in me! Oh God, I had no intention of riding a go-kart but I had to, or else Jaden would be left out.

I asked the girl at the counter what I needed to know about riding the go-kart. I was told, "The green pedal is the accelerator and the red pedal is the brake, and then you just steer!" Right.

As we got in the two-seater kart, I was trying to figure out what to do with my large tote purse. I tried to shift my body to make room for the purse. I had no idea that the kart was already *running*. As the attendant came to fasten Jaden's seat belt, I accidentally tapped the accelerator and the kart lunged forward!! I almost cut off the guy's arm!

I was so embarrassed and apologized profusely. He just gritted his teeth and didn't say anything. I'm sure he was calling me various names and obscenities under his breath. I felt awful. Do you think they could have told me it wasn't like an amusement park ride where it doesn't "go" until they flip a switch?

We went around the track maybe 8 times and Jaden was laughing with delight.

When the buzzer signaled the end of the laps, we pulled into our lane and Jaden jumped out of our kart, as did the girls from their go-karts. They ran off to the arcade and left me sitting in my kart. I was afraid that if I pushed myself up,

I might step on the accelerator again, and "we" didn't want that to happen. The attendant made no attempt to help me out. I understood I was on my own.

There was a dad in the kart behind me (a strong black man about 40) who had been riding with his son. He came over and offered his strong arm to pull me out. Oh God. So embarrassing. This is why a 64-year-old grandma should never ride a go-kart without a second adult to pull you out.

The rest of the afternoon was uneventful. The kids cheated at miniature golf and won hundreds of tickets at the arcade, which resulted in a prize worth about 10 cents. But they were happy and had a good time.

Grandma was quite relieved to get back home, but the go-kart ride made for a great Facebook post!

Elly's Follies, Las Vegas

I SPENT THE ENTIRE DAY packing and checking things off my list to pack for our trip to Las Vegas to visit my cousin Bonnie and her husband Bill. We just had a few last-minute essentials to slip into the bags the next morning, like our pills and my charged phone. I put the Southwest boarding passes for the flight to Chicago in my carry-on.

At 7 p.m., I realized there was no room left in my carry-on bag for my new "DOGBONE™ Bone Pillow." I never leave home without it, at least not for trips. So, I unpacked some things from the carry-on bag, such as the AAA book, street maps, a novel, and a pair of dress shoes, and slipped them into my suitcase. The pillow finally fit.

I took half of a Tylenol PM to help me sleep. I fell asleep right away but awakened at 12:30, unable to fall back to sleep, excited about the trip. After a mere 3 hours sleep, I got up at 3 a.m. I felt like a zombie.

I fed the cat, left out extra dry food, freshened two bowls of water, spruced up the bathroom, took an Airborne, and kissed my kitty Natasha goodbye. She would be well taken care of by my friend Judy Caysinger.

We drove to Eric's house. The plan was that he would drop us off at the airport and drive my car into work, then leave the car in Short-Term Parking on the day of our return. I'd keep my keys. On the way to the airport, I asked Eric if he had my extra set of keys. He had forgotten them. So, Plan B was that he'd have to pick us up from the airport when we returned.

Check-in was relatively easy. The first two bags were free—yay! I looked on my ticket and saw that it was marked TSA Pre, which meant I could go right through security without taking out my liquids or removing my shoes. Jeff had to wait in the long line, and he also had to be x-rayed, rather than scanned because of his ICD (pacemaker/defibrillator). I waited for him at the gate.

As I was sitting there, I thought I would check our boarding passes for the Chicago-to-Las Vegas leg of the trip. I opened my carry-on bag and my heart sunk. The boarding passes were in the AAA book I moved to my suitcase! I panicked. I think my blood pressure read "tilt."

I went up to the gate attendant, who was very kind and prompt to print out another copy. WHEW!

We arrived in Las Vegas about 11:25 a.m. Pacific Time. Gosh, I was tired! It felt like 9 p.m. for me. We followed the signs for Baggage, which led us to a tram. We just followed the crowd because we didn't have a clue where we were going. We also followed the crowd to the baggage area. Before we got to the carousel, Bonnie and Bill appeared with big smiles and hugs. Bonnie had just won $8 on the slot machine that paid for their parking.

I was amazed at the Las Vegas landscape. I guess I didn't expect mountains! I thought it was all desert. We had about a half-hour drive to Bonnie's house, and we got to see the

Strip in the distance and all the unique southwest design and architecture along the way.

Bonnie showed us around her 4-bedroom, 3-bath hacienda, including our bedroom for the week. When we saw the twin beds, I thought, *"Lucy and Ricky's bedroom!"* Jeff thought, *"WTF."*

Bonnie made us tuna sandwiches for lunch. I wanted to crawl into bed, but forced myself to stay awake. We unpacked and relaxed on their patio, which was lovely.

We watched as hummingbirds buzzed in the sycamore trees. It was amazing! The people in back of her had a bullmastiff—Ruger. He kept jumping up on the wall and barking at us. They had three other dogs including a poodle, and another neighbor had four dogs. One of them was always barking morning to night.

As Bonnie made a chicken gumbo for dinner, she was adding some cayenne pepper and I heard her say, "Oops!" A "little" too much went in. After she tasted the gumbo, her lips went numb! She added a lot of rice, but it didn't help very much. It was so hot, I could barely eat it, even though I did. She gave Jeff a second helping. He offered no resistance. She apologized for trying to kill us.

I went to bed at 9 p.m. I had been up for 21 hours and was beyond exhausted.

I woke at 4:30 a.m., after 8 hours of sleep. I wandered into the kitchen in my nightgown and found the light. I did a crossword puzzle and a Jumble, and read a couple chapters in my book. Around 6:30, after it was light, I decided to go out and get the paper. There was no alarm, and Bonnie told me where to find the paper.

It was a double-lock door. I turned the top lock and then the bottom lock, and opened the door. I was afraid that Bill's cat, Cali, would run out, so I closed the door behind me.

It was a glorious morning. I found the paper and walked back to the door. It was locked!! I thought I must be imagining it because I clearly unlocked both locks. I tried again. I shook the door. Nothing. Crap. I opened the paper and read a section, then tried knocking on the door. No response. I tried every five minutes. Nada. I rang the doorbell. No answer. I rapped on a window, but it was in a side room. I rang the bell two more times and knocked loudly. I had been out there about 30 minutes in my nightgown. Finally, Bill heard the bell and came to the door. Apparently, they never use the top lock on the door, which re-locked when the door closed. sigh.

Later, the four of us drove to Spring Preserve, a southwest botanical garden and butterfly habitat. The temperature was 91°. We paid upfront for the garden, but the butterfly habitat was extra. The girl informed us that there were just a couple of butterflies, and asked if we could come back on Thursday when a new shipment of butterflies would come in! Really?? Not after paying 20 bucks to get in! We did enjoy the two butterfly species that were there.

We skipped lunch and had an early dinner at the Santa Fe Station casino buffet. Bonnie was big on discounts and coupons so we saved a lot. There was the senior discount, the military discount, and the local discount, plus a BOGO coupon. Cost=$4.32 per person. We couldn't go wrong!

After dark, we checked out the Bellagio casino and fountains and all the lights on the Strip. Throngs of people! And girls with thongs! and fans! tsk, tsk.

Bonnie also showed us how to understand the slot machine costs. She gave me $5 to play (since I just had a $20 and I didn't want to part with it). I left with 40 cents. I never played again.

The next day, Bonnie and Bill said they had been warned about Fremont Street, the original Las Vegas Strip, from their cop friend. "Don't go there. If you do, watch out for pickpockets." Bonnie really didn't want to risk it. However, Jeff and I convinced her to go during daylight hours. It was certainly no worse than Yonge Street in Toronto or the French Quarter in New Orleans.

Fremont Street was under a dome, and the only cars were on cross streets. There were famous casinos like the Golden Nugget, souvenir shops, ziplining, showgirls in skimpy clothes, street bars, street vendors and performers, and restaurants.

Fremont Street, Las Vegas

Just off Fremont Street was the Mob Museum—my favorite place in Vegas! Very well done, intriguing, and lots of interactive stations. There was even a quick mention of Rochester, NY, in a slide show in the actual courtroom where the mobsters were tried and convicted.

On Friday, the guys got up early and went to a hot rod "meet" in a nearby plaza. Jeff got to ride in Bill's hot rod. Then we headed for the Las Vegas Strip.

We walked from the Mirage parking lot to the south end of Caesar's Palace. Bill chose to stay behind in Caesar's while we checked out some of the strip. It's a good thing. It was really hot and the crowds were crazy. Plus, there was a broken escalator and we had to walk up 40 steps. ugh. Bonnie suffered with her asthma.

We went to the Flamingo where we saw the birds and beautiful waterfalls, Caesar's where we walked through the day-to-night skies and saw the moving statues, and the Venetian where we saw the gondola ride (we didn't go on it).

At dinner time, we drove to the Wynn where we celebrated Bonnie and Bill's 9th anniversary at the garden buffet. We treated them for all their hospitality. After dinner, we wandered around the Wynn and Jeff gambled $20. He left with 60 cents.

Jeff, Bonnie, and I went to see the Terry Fator show at The Mirage. It was a last-minute decision for Bonnie so she didn't sit with us. She got the front row to the side.

The opening DJ was great and got us all moving. The 90-minute show was excellent, and I laughed so hard my face hurt. Terry did fantastic impressions of Michael Jackson and the Beatles. The proceeds at the gift shop all went to the Wounded Warriors Project. So honorable!

The day before we left Vegas, I printed off ALL our boarding passes and put them in my carry-on bag.

Bill gave me a ride in his hot rod. So cool!

It was still dark when Bill and Bonnie drove us to the airport at 4:30 a.m. We saw the Strip lit up from a distance. The flight was very short, and we arrived in Rochester just about on time. There was a very long wait at the baggage carousel, but Eric was outside with Amanda waiting for us and we hopped in right away.

It was so good to be home and hug my kitty. We found this note on the front door, "Welcome Home, Mom & Dad! I've been a VERY GOOD GIRL! But I missed you a lot! I heard rumors 'bout you in Vegas, but I love you anyway. Natasha"

Natasha started meowing when we walked in and then stopped, in shock, to see us standing there and not Judy. Haha.

Coat Caper

I AM A KNUCKLEHEAD, pure and simple. By now, you know it, too. This will prove it.

I went to get my teeth cleaned, and the hygienist who was checking my teeth said, "Do you have thrush or something? There are spots all over your throat. Not your tongue; just your throat."

Holy crap! I had no idea, but I was diagnosed with thrush in the past, after using a steroid inhaler. My dentist came in and confirmed it. He asked me to contact my physician and get a script.

I went to the front desk to pay my bill and then walked over to Jeff who was sitting in the waiting room. He got up and put his jacket on and I knew my new turquoise winter coat was next to his jacket so I grabbed it and we left. I didn't bother to zip it.

Since my primary physician, Dr. Meloni, was a mile down the road, we drove to his office and I asked his secretary to have him send in a script. I gave her my cell number.

We drove to Papa Joe's Italian Restaurant to meet Jeff's friends and their wives for a Christmas lunch. On the way, I held my brand-new iPhone in my hand, expecting the doctor to call or to get a text from my pharmacy saying my script was ready. Then I realized that the cell phone clearly said "No Service." Because the phone was new, there was no way for the doctor or the pharmacy to call me. I had to go to AT&T first and have them reset the SIM card. I couldn't make any calls either or text or check the internet. I hoped that, by the time lunch was done, the script would be ready.

When we got to Papa Joe's, I decided to hang my coat in the vestibule. Mike, Jeff's buddy, helped me as I took it off and he hung it up for me. We stayed at the restaurant until 2:30 (when they close for two hours) and had a great time. The ladies exchanged gifts so we all ooh'd and aah'd over everything. When it was time to go, I went to the vestibule to get my coat, but it wasn't there! My brand-new winter coat was GONE. Mike insisted that the coat left on the rack was mine (because he hung it there), but it was NOT my coat. I was very confused. I assumed my new coat was stolen (or taken by mistake). I would have called 911, except that I couldn't make a call on my iPhone. And now I was going to freeze my ass off. I gave the owner my name and phone number in case the person who "took my coat by mistake" returned it.

We drove to the AT&T store where Jeff left me off at the door and I scurried inside, shivering. I told them I was having a bad day and that someone stole my coat. After we chatted, they reset my SIM card and my iPhone now had service. I called Wegmans and asked them about the script and they said they'd have it ready for me shortly. Jeff dropped me off at the door of Wegmans, and once again, scurried inside to pick up the script. I froze walking back to the car in the parking lot.

We were just about 8 miles from our house when the dentist's office called. I was expecting my doctor to call, but not my dentist. I thought, *"Maybe they are just checking on my thrush."* The receptionist asked, "By any chance did you take the wrong coat by mistake?" Honest to God, it still didn't hit me. I told them that someone took my coat at the restaurant. They didn't know what to say.

As I thought more about it, I wondered if I took somebody else's coat at the dentist's office. So, I called the dentist's office back and asked if their missing coat was turquoise. They said they didn't know and would call me back, which they did. Yes, the lady said she had a turquoise coat. OMG, she put it next to Jeff's coat and I just grabbed it, thinking it was mine! The poor lady had to leave without a coat in the freezing temps. And when I arrived at Papa Joe's, Mike took my coat and I never looked at it. Then after lunch, I didn't see MY coat because it wasn't there! I felt like a complete jackass, which I was.

So, I had to call Papa Joe's and explain the mix-up. Because it was late and Papa Joe's was closed, and I was 40 miles away, I had to return there the next day at 11:30, pick up the coat, then drive back to my dentist's and turn it in. I also bought a gift for the lady and put it in a Christmas gift bag, which I hoped she'd accept with my apologies. The receptionist did say that people have taken the wrong coat from the rack more times than she can remember. That made me feel a little better.

"Serenity now!"

Close to Death

IT WAS THE WORST OF YEARS. It was the best of years.

I came down with viral bronchitis and laryngitis on February 11, 2018. I went to Urgent Care where I had an x-ray (which was clear) and was prescribed a rescue inhaler, then followed up with Dr. Meloni, my primary doctor, who concurred with the diagnosis. On March 21, I coughed for 12 hours straight, and by 5 a.m., I was having trouble breathing. I woke Jeff and told him, gasping, to drive me to the ER in Brockport, NY.

Instead of pulling up to the ER door, he parked somewhere in the lot. I was having difficulty walking because oxygen wasn't getting to my lungs. He kept coaxing me along until I walked in the doors and flopped myself down in a wheelchair. The receptionist was shocked and got me into a bed asap. They treated me with oxygen and albuterol and did an x-ray. My lungs were still clear. An ambulance took me to Highland Hospital where I stayed for 4 days and was put on Prednisone. I was diagnosed with Respiratory Distress due to a blocked airway (mucus plug). I was assigned a home aide and was "homebound" for three weeks.

On April 4, I was eating dinner (actually, choking on dinner because of my intense cough), when the phone rang and Caller ID said Joe Janowicz. I thought I was hallucinating! *"Wha? Why is he calling?"* I wondered. I jumped up, pushed the furniture aside, did a cartwheel and a somersault, and grabbed the phone. Not really, but that's what it felt like to hear from someone you haven't seen since the 1990s. He said he got my number from the Town Supervisor, his brother-in-law, and asked if I would be willing to edit a novel for him! I said sure in my croaking voice. As sick as I was, I could still edit. We worked 10 months on the book, *Bang-Bang You're Dead,* and it really helped me to focus on something other than my illness and get well. Not only that; it was fun, too. And since neither one of us had ever worked on a book before, it was a learning experience with its ups and downs.

On April 19, the day I was "discharged" from the home-aide service, Jeff and I went to Walmart for cough medicine, when I developed severe breathing problems again. What the heck! I had to leave the store immediately. Jeff drove me home but I couldn't get out of the car. He called 911. I truly thought I was going to die. However, I wasn't seeing ghosts of my mother or Grandma Littlebetter, so, I thought, maybe I wasn't going to die after all. But I thought the ambulance would never come! I did tell the EMT that I was going to die, but he said, "Not on my watch!" He saved my life with an albuterol mask which cleared my airway.

The ambulance took me to Unity Hospital, lights and sirens going, because it was the closest place and I was seriously ill. I was diagnosed with Respiratory Failure with Hypoxia, as oxygen was not reaching my organs and they could fail and I could die. I also had a stress-induced "heart attack" and had to wear a heart monitor. They did a CT scan with contrast (clear), an angiogram (my arteries were totally clear), and an echocardiogram (no damage). I did have fluid buildup around my heart so I was put on a diuretic and a beta blocker. I was told that my heart would return to normal in a few weeks, and it did. I was hospitalized for 4 days then went home.

In June, I still had laryngitis and a new symptom—sinus blockage. Patty threw a 50th wedding anniversary party for Jeff and me that was beyond anything I dreamed of! (Eric also helped financially.) What a great job she did! Seventy family and close friends showed up from all over the U.S., and everyone had a great time and enjoyed the food at Red Fedele's Brook House. I wished I had felt better to enjoy it more, but it will always be memorable and dear to my heart.

A few weeks later, the ENT doctor had to drill through my stuffed nose. They tried to numb it first, but the numbing spray went right back into the physician assistant's face! With an entry to my sinuses, they finally were able to use the spray and check everything with a scope. After 16 days on Prednisone (again), my nose was clear and I had a CT scan. My deviated septum wasn't bad enough to have surgery. I went to an allergist who tested me for environmental allergies. My only allergies were dust mites and cock-roaches! By *December* (10 months later), the bronchitis seemed to be gone, but the sinus blockage was back, so I returned to the ENT and the allergist. They put me on Prednisone again for 16 days.

My health has been a real roller-coaster ride, especially with sinus and ear issues, which I continue to deal with.

As I said earlier, 2018 was the worst of years (close to death); yet it was the best of years (editing Joe's book and starting my own book). I really believe that someone "on the other side" was looking out for me. Working with Joe really helped me through a very tough year and it was extremely rewarding for me by doing what I truly loved—editing and writing.

My Search for Serenity

OVER THE YEARS, MY QUEST HAS been for "serenity." But to find serenity, I discovered that first you must have drama and stress in your life. It's how you handle the chaos and rise above it. I choose laughter. I've done some silly things that have gotten me into trouble and I've had my share of sorrow, but when you can laugh about your mistakes and embarrassing moments and remember all the funny things that you, or your loved ones, have done, you've gained acceptance and peace. Serenity has been there all the time, like an old friend with a hand on your shoulder.

Thanks to my husband Jeff and all my family and friends for a lifetime of memories. And thanks to Joe Janowicz for believing in me and encouraging me to write.

I encourage you to tell or write down your stories for your children and grandchildren so they will know what life was like for you.

Now, here are a few stories from my sisters—Marcia and Patty—that I hope you will enjoy.

Sincerely,

Elly

The Baumann Street gang—
my funny brother Mickey, beautiful sister Patty,
darling husband Jeff, me, talented sister Marcia,
super-smart son Eric, and sweet (ex) sister-in-law Debbie.
"Nerd Party" 1982.

Marcia's Stories

Rochester, NY

Not the Best Behavior

IT WAS THE LAW IN our Catholic grammar school, Our Lady of Perpetual Help, that all grades one through eight attend the Children's Mass at 8:15 every Sunday during the school term, under pain of being "murdalized" by your teacher. The teachers were nuns who put Marine drill sergeants to shame once riled. According to accepted order, girls occupied the front pews for each class and boys behind them, followed by the teacher. Parents occupied the back pews in the church.

One particular Sunday when I was in third grade, I ended up in the pew right in front of the boys. I laid my little purse on the seat next to me, but when I reached for it, the boy behind me informed me that he had my purse and wasn't going to give it back. This led to an argument of whispers.

"Give it back!" I whispered as I gave him the evil eye.

"No!" he said, taunting me.

"Give it back!" I ordered again, with my teeth clenched.

"No!" he said defiantly.

I was so distraught that I stood up on the seat with one leg over the back of the pew, ready to beat up the thief, or at least punch his face in.

Now, all this was going on during Mass when we were expected to observe the service with some solemnity and decorum. The next thing I knew, the teacher, Sister Germana, was running down the aisle toward me, with Mom close behind. Due to their intervention, I soon had my purse back and the thief was in the state of subjection.

Afterwards, Mom said, "Are you nuts? We could have gotten your purse later." She was dreadfully embarrassed.

Sister Germana wasn't so kind. She promised the thief that a punishment was on its way, and she informed me in no uncertain terms that climbing over the pew during the Mass in order to beat up the person behind me was not acceptable behavior.

Due to my own embarrassment, I draw down the curtain on what followed the next day...

Squirrel Encounter

MOM ALWAYS HAD GOOD intentions by warning me of the dangers of daily life and I'm sure she didn't mean to make me a quaking, paranoid wreck, which I am to this day.

"Do not go down Laser Street because there are bad people there!"

"Do not talk to strangers because they may kidnap and murder you!"

"Why don't you hang around with Margaret (an Irish girl) and not Mary Ann (an Italian girl)?"

"Italians carry knives and will stab you." I have known and loved Italian friends and have yet to be stabbed. Mom loved Irish folk and wasn't crazy about anyone else.

She also lectured me on squirrels.

"Don't go near squirrels because they will attack and bite you and you might get rabies!" Mom warned.

One afternoon, shortly after her warning, Mom and I were sitting on our open front porch, enjoying a summer's day when, all of a sudden, a squirrel hopped up on the porch and came toward us.

Because it was so soon after her dire warning, we both started screaming, as if we were in mortal danger. The poor squirrel paused, took one look at us two "looney tunes," and said to himself, "Okay, I'm outta here," and off he went. Neighbors were looking out their front doors to see if Baumann Street was under attack.

Dad came running out of the house and asked loudly, "What's going on?"

When we told him about the squirrel, he said a few choice words and told us that all the neighbors were thinking that someone was being murdered at our house.

Our neighbors soon realized, "Oh, it's only the crazy Fedyks," and went back inside.

Dad, not known for putting things delicately nor of mincing words, said, "Of course the squirrel came on the porch. He was after the two nuts!"

Father Newcomb
Looks Out for the Fedyks

FATHER NEWCOMB, ASSISTANT priest at OLPH, was a dear, sweet man. The only problem was that he couldn't hear too well.

We were told to go to confession once a month so Ma would troop in with me and Jimmy on a Saturday afternoon, but one thing she didn't want to do was go to Fr. Newcomb's confessional. Two confessionals were permanently installed on either side of the church, but Fr. Newcomb's confessional was a portable one in the middle aisle. The problem was, when you went to that one, Fr. Newcomb talked loudly and you had to tell your sins loudly so that he could hear you. When you left the confessional, if everyone was laughing or grinning, you knew that they heard how many times you hit your kids, swore at them, or worse. Needless to say, people avoided this confessional, especially Ma.

One Saturday Ma said, "Let's sit in the back so that I don't have to go to Fr. Newcomb." But Fr. Newcomb came out looking for "customers" and spotted Ma.

"Alright, Helen. Come on," he hollered to her. Everybody turned to look at us.

"He wants you, Ma. Go for it!" I was laughing at this point but now she had no choice but to go.

When she got in the confessional, I could hear him say, "How are you, Helen?" I heard her try to mumble her confession but she came out all red in the face. She said, "Oh, I'm so embarrassed!"

I assured her that I couldn't hear what she said but I thought it was pretty funny.

* * * * *

When Ma took us to Sunday Mass, for reasons unknown to us, she always sat in the front pew in front of the pulpit. Ma was always trying to give us good example by acting very pious. She knelt very straight and looked like she was in a prayerful trance. The only problem was us three "rascally rabbits"—me, Jimmy, and Ella. We poked and harassed each other behind her back all through Mass. Once in a while she would "come to" and give us a swat, much to the relief of the people around us.

One summer, during the week before Sunday Mass, I told Jimmy and little Ella, "If you get bored during Mass, focus your eyes on one object and everything around it will disappear." But, if anyone looked at us, it would seem that we were cross-eyed.

Apparently, we were all bored that Sunday during the sermon given by Fr. Newcomb. After Mass, he stopped us as we exited the church. He said to Ma, "I never realized that your kids are cross-eyed."

"WHAT?" Ma said. "Cross-eyed?"

Later on, she looked at all of us and said, "You're not cross-eyed. What is he talking about?"

So about then we all fessed up in our own way and Ma said, "Oh, for crying out loud. You kids will be the death of me."

Patty's Stories

Victor, NY

Gun Safety Course

MY 12-YEAR-OLD SON, ALEX, wanted to hunt so badly but, in order to do that, he needed to take a gun safety course. One little problem: Alex had a bit of anxiety about taking the course by himself. It was a two-day weekend course on East Lake Road in the hills above Honeoye Lake, NY. In order to make him more comfortable, I told him that I would go with him and hang out in class.

It was a long, snowy drive in my minivan—longer than I expected. I found the driveway and slowly meandered up an icy, tree-lined hill. Not far up the incline, my tires started spinning. I could not go any farther. I tentatively backed down, knowing my son was worried. Once we reached the bottom, we discussed how to get up the driveway and then decided to walk. I hiked halfway up and determined I couldn't go any farther. I have a problem with my heart's rhythm and it was really acting up that day.

Alex tried to convince me to continue, and I tried to convince Alex to go without me. We both refused to budge.

Finally, someone from the top of the hill arrived in a four-wheeler-type vehicle with a caged seating area. They gave a really embarrassed mom a ride up to the top of the hill.

We entered the taxidermy-lined foyer filled with animals such as zebra and antelope. My first instinct was to pet the zebra but was admonished by Alex, who pointed at a DO NOT TOUCH sign. Oops. Alex was amazed by the display of guns including assault rifles.

Once the class began, the instructor noticed that I was not enrolled and convinced me to take the class since I was there anyway. Being the only woman, I wanted to prove that I could do it. It was interesting and informative, including learning how to shoot a gun and drop and roll with one.

During class, we heard that some other classmates' cars slid down the driveway and one even hit a police car driven by a guest instructor. The class took a break while they made a few calls and inspected the damage.

The snow did not abate while we were attending class. On the way home, we barely made it up Route 20A leaving Honeoye going towards Bristol. Classmates passed us as we struggled up the hill.

The second day's drive and arrival were uneventful. As we left, I said, "Good thing we didn't drive to the top yesterday. Look at that gully!" The sides of the driveway were lined with stick-like trees too small to stop a sliding car from careening into the ravine.

I am happy to say that Alex and I passed with high marks!

Just Another Crazy Weekend
At the McGraw's

IT SEEMED LIKE my sons, Ryan and Alex, liked to have friends over most weekends. Alex invited a new friend to our home to hang out and sleep over. He was very tall and lean and was very polite.

They decided they wanted to walk around the nearby mall for a while. As I drove them to the mall, I noticed a car pulled over to the side of the road, and someone leaning on his car looking "unsure." I stopped next to him and asked if he needed help. He did and I offered to give him a lift.

I waited for him while to get his things and he slid into the back seat of my minivan...with pizza boxes! I asked him if he was delivering pizzas when he broke down. After an affirmative answer, what else could I do? With a totally mortified son, I drove to the next housing development and delivered the pizzas. After driving the thankful boy back to the pizza shop, I thought, "I should have asked for the tip!"

When the boys were ready to leave the mall, I picked them up and drove past a car on the side of the road with another unsure driver. My son yelled at me not to stop! He was really embarrassed in front of his new friend. Well, I had to do it. I asked if he needed help and, luckily for Alex, the kid was just waiting for his mom.

The next day was a little crazy, too. Alex and his friend walked in the woods behind our house. There were some marshy areas and Alex became stuck up to his knees. After several attempts by his new friend, he was freed. Both were muddy past their knees and came in to change. Alex let his friend borrow some sweat pants but they were too short. The poor kid had to walk around the rest of the day wearing knickers!

Needless to say, his friend never came back.

Cleaning Day

ALEX AND MY HUSBAND Tim were at a baseball tournament one weekend, and I thought it was a good time to catch up on some much-needed upper-level cleaning.

I turned off the TV and began scrubbing the upstairs bathroom. I realized I needed glass cleaner so I went downstairs to retrieve it. I heard voices that made me stop in my tracks.

"It can't be the TV," I thought. I knew that I had turned it off. I slowly went in the living room. Only my dog Toby was there sleeping on the couch. I heard the voices speaking again, except now I could hear what they were saying. Let's just say that it was obviously inappropriate. The TV was off...but it sounded like it was coming from the receiver. (My husband has the TV/cable hooked up through the receiver.) Could it be that it was picking up my neighbors' private moments!?! Egad!

I quickly pressed buttons and tried to change it. The screen came on and the guide showed it was tuned into a porn movie! (The name will not be mentioned.) I turned and looked for the remote. Where was it? Toby sat up and revealed the remote.

Shame on you, Toby!

The worst part...I called the cable company to remove the charges and explained that my dog ordered the porn. I don't think they believed me.

The Milk Lady

I OFTEN WOULD TAKE my dog Toby through our town's neighborhoods to look for squirrels so that he could have a good bark. One day, while "squirreling," I saw a woman in her 60s filling a bird feeder in her front yard. I thought, *"That will be me someday."*

Strangely, I continued to see her everywhere. I saw her at church, at a senior living facility in a neighboring town, and at various other places.

As I was leaving our local grocery store, the same woman walked up to me and handed me a gallon of milk, saying, "Here, this is for you." I was dumbfounded and mumbled something in reply as she walked away.

I took my groceries home and recanted the story to my teenage son, Alex, who was immediately suspicious. He insisted that I test for pinholes in case she poisoned it. After a few minutes of squeezing and tipping, we determined it was safe to drink.

I never saw her again.

Ryan's Bad Day

RYAN MOWED LAWNS FOR A few neighbors. One day he just had rotten luck.

He normally mows for our next-door neighbor who has a lot that borders a field. Ryan would mow one strip of it along a ditch. This day he went a little too far and got stuck.

He tried everything and finally came to get me. I tried to push him out but could not. A truck with two men stopped to see if we needed help. Of course, we said yes!

Ryan hopped on the mower and they pushed and rocked him out of the ditch. I thanked them but noticed they looked distressed. It was only when I saw them hopping up and down and slapping their legs that I realized they had been standing on a very large ant hill. The agitated ants were crawling all over their legs!

Ryan moved on to our yard and unfortunately ran out of gas. He didn't have far to go for the gas tank but he was interrupted by stinging sensations. He ran out of gas right under a hornets' nest hanging from our deck! He still remembers the bees stinging him over and over again!

Chickens in the Foyer

ALEX INFORMED ME THAT it was his turn to bring the classroom chickens home for the weekend. Oh boy!

We didn't know where to put them. I was told that they did not fly. They were still very young, so we kept them in a box in the foyer.

Our next-door neighbor's son came over to look at them. The poor kid had a cast on his leg due to a broken ankle. As he was observing them, a chicken flew up and landed on his head! He started screaming and clunking his cast around the room with the chicken firmly planted on his head. He was terrified!

Well, I guess young chickens can fly after all.

Toby Makes Change

OUR TOWN HAS A YEARLY festival and on this particular year they were having a pet contest. Residents brought their furry loved ones to show off their talents.

They asked each of us to tell us what their pets could do. My dog Toby did not have many skills, so I was at a loss. I told them that Toby could make change. They were astounded until I told them how he made change. One day he ate a five-dollar bill and pooped out change!

He won.

Made in the USA
Columbia, SC
08 March 2020

88659114R00163